FAMOUS FIRSTS
OF BLACK WOMEN

FAMOUS FIRSTS ——OF—— BLACK WOMEN

Martha Ward Plowden

Illustrated by Ronald Jones

Second Edition

PELICAN PUBLISHING COMPANY
Gretna 2002

First printing, October 1993
Second printing, November 1994
Second edition, January 2002

*Many thanks to Mrs. Annie M. Ward and Ms. Annie Pauline Ward.
Love and many thanks also to Nathaniel and Natalie
for their support and understanding.*

---

*The word "Pelican" and the depiction of a pelican are
trademarks of Pelican Publishing Company, Inc., and are
registered in the U.S. Patent and Trademark Office.*

Library of Congress Cataloging-in-Publication

Plowden, Martha Ward.
Famous firsts of Black women / Martha Ward Plowden ; illustrated by Ronald Jones.
p. cm.
Includes bibliographical references.
Summary: Focuses on notable African-American women who have helped shape
American destiny, including contributors in the fields of politics, sports, and the arts.
ISBN 1-56554-197-9
1. African American women—History—Juvenile literature. 2. African American
women—Biography—Juvenile literature. [1. African Americans—History. 2. African
Americans—Biography. 3. Women—History. 4. Women—Biography.] I. Jones, Ronald
(Ronald Leonard), 1952- ill. II. Title.

E185.86 .P58 2002
305.48'896073—dc21

2001036657

Printed in the United States of America

Published by Pelican Publishing Company, Inc.
1000 Burmaster Street, Gretna, Louisiana 70053

To my late father,
Rev. Isiah Paul Ward, Sr.

CONTENTS

PREFACE

Famous Firsts of Black Women gives information about African-American women, from slavery to the present, who have set precedents and made various contributions to this country. These women have played a major role in defining and shaping American beliefs and culture.

These individuals were selected for this book based on the following criteria: being an African-American female and being recognized as the first in her area or field. Some are well known and their lives and works have been dealt with extensively, but there are others with very little information available on their accomplishments. Many of these individuals have overcome incredible hardships with little to sustain them but their own courage and determination.

This book is designed to provide a record of African-American women who struggled against the odds, using every strategy available, to achieve greatness in an impressive number of fields.

FAMOUS FIRSTS
OF BLACK WOMEN

Opera Singer

Marian Anderson

MARIAN ANDERSON
(Born 1902—Died 1993)

Marian Anderson was the first African-American woman to win first prize in a voice contest, sponsored by the Philadelphia Harmonic Society in 1923. Two years later, competing against 300 singers in New York City, she won the Lewisohn Stadium Concert Award and appeared with the New York Philharmonic Orchestra at the stadium on August 26, 1925. A few years after that she received a Rosenwald Foundation Fellowship, enabling her to go to Germany, where she studied the *Lieder* (German songs) that were to be, along with spirituals, such an important part of her repertoire.

At the peak of her career, Ms. Anderson was considered the world's greatest contralto. When she made her Town Hall debut in New York on December 31, 1935, Howard Taubman, reviewer for *The New York Times*, described it as "music-making that probed too deep for words."

Marian grew up in South Philadelphia. She was born on February 17, 1902 and she was the oldest of three girls. Her family was poor but they were close and had a lot of love, so Marian never thought of herself as being deprived. Among the things she never had as a young child were professional music lessons. Even though her family was aware that she had a rare talent, they could not afford the voice training they knew she should have. From the age of six Marian sang in the choir at the Union Baptist Church, where her father carried her every Sunday. The weekly practice gave her invaluable training. It not only introduced her to the deep spirituality of music but it also gave her the ability to sing with ease in front of large audiences. Singing in the Union Baptist choir gave Marian a unique opportunity to develop her extraordinary voice range. Each week she carried home the music and practiced all the parts, so she was always prepared to fill in if someone was absent. Marian's voice was classified by musicians as contralto. She could reach up to the high soprano notes, and even down to the low music of the baritone.

When Marian was about eight years old, her father bought a piano from his brother. Marian was delighted with the instrument. There was no money for lessons, but with the help of a card marked with the notes, she taught herself to play some simple songs. Marian got the urge to play the violin, after seeing one in the window of a pawnshop. She saved up the pennies and nickels she earned from scrubbing her neighbors' steps after school so she could buy the violin for $3.98. A friend of the family taught her how to tune the violin and to play a few notes. But before long the strings snapped and the wood of the violin cracked.

Marian's father died suddenly, so Marian, her mother, and her two sisters had to move in with her father's parents. Her mother helped support the family by working as a cleaning woman and a laundress, while her grandmother took care of the girls at home.

Marian's mother's quiet strength and deep faith were to be the enduring influences in her life. As she grew older, she began to realize that the only limit to her success was the color of her skin. But the strength from which she drew her unfailing calm was the rich heritage of her mother, who taught her well the quiet power of believing, simply believing that right would be done, that when one way was barred another would be found. Her mother also taught her the importance of hard work in achieving goals. Even as a young girl, Marian added to the family income by scrubbing porch steps, a job she undertook with the same intensity and thoroughness that she was later to give to her professional training.

That training began when she was still in high school. A

16

neighbor, whose voice Marian greatly admired, gave her free lessons. Secretly Marian dreamed of becoming a singer when she grew up.

People all over Philadelphia got to know about her magnificent voice. They asked her to perform at their parties and club meetings. While still in high school, Marian was getting five dollars every time she sang at one of these affairs.

Marian was encouraged to transfer from William Penn High School to a music school in South Philadelphia. She was more shocked than humiliated when she was dismissed with a single sentence. "We don't take colored," the woman said coldly, and turned away.

Marian told her mother that the statement bit into her soul, and she asked her mother if it was wrong to think that an African-American girl could become a singer. Were her dreams foolish? Her mother reassured her that she could become a singer, but she must have faith.

Her mother also taught her that you can't do anything by yourself. There is always somebody to make the stone flat for you to stand on. This time it was the African-American community of Philadelphia, people who had heard her sing in their churches.

The people at Union Baptist Church had confidence in Marian's talent. These friends and neighbors planned a concert to help her. All the money received from the concert was set aside to pay for a year's worth of private singing lessons for Marian with Agnes Reifsnyder. Marian performed at the concert herself, but the main star was Roland Hayes. Mr. Hayes was the first African-American singer to become famous in the concert halls of America and Europe. From this time on, Marian's pride, faith, and hope began to grow.

At age nineteen Marian began studying with Giuseppe Boghetti. When Mr. Boghetti thought Marian was ready, he allowed her to enter a contest of 300 young singers. The first prize was a chance to perform with the New York Philharmonic Orchestra. By now Marian's voice was well trained and she put her whole spirit into the music. After she sang, the other contestants clapped and cheered. Then the judges announced that she had won.

Marian had hoped that this prize would prove she was ready to sing in America's best concert halls. But most Americans just did not want to believe that an African-American could be an excellent concert singer. Marian felt that her career was not progressing, so after a short engagement with the Philadelphia Symphony Orchestra, she decided to go to Europe, where she would study with famous singing masters on a scholarship granted by the National Association of Negro Musicians.

She studied first in England, then she went to Germany, where she met Kosti Vehamen, who became her accompanist. Together they toured the Scandinavian countries. In these countries Marian was accepted as a great singer by everyone who heard her. It did not matter to these people that Marian was African-American and most of them were white, because they loved her voice and they loved her. During her tour of Europe she met Arturo Toscanini, the famous orchestra conductor. He came to one of her concerts and was so impressed with her singing that he went backstage and said to her that a voice like hers is "heard once in a hundred years."

Though she was a success on the concert tour and with the New York Philharmonic, Marian realized that her opportunities in the United States were limited because of her color. She then toured Europe again, meeting with more critical acclaim. On that highly successful tour, she performed before the crowned heads of state in a number of countries.

Marian's stay in Europe helped her find her place as a singer, but it was time to return home to America, where her family was. On the ocean liner she had an accident and broke a bone in her foot. But Marian did not disappoint the people who came to the concert December 31, 1935 at Town Hall in New York. During the next thirty years Marian sang all over the world.

In the spring of 1939 Marian planned to give a concert in Washington, D.C., the nation's capital. She hoped to appear in Constitution Hall. It was owned by the Daughters of the

American Revolution, a group of women whose families had long ago fought for freedom in the United States. The D.A.R. refused to let Marian sing on their stage, because she was an African-American. Marian was not a fighter, but through her music she would do whatever she could to gain freedom and justice for her people. Leaders of the United States government invited her to give her concert outdoors at the Lincoln Memorial on Easter Sunday. She stood before the statue of Abraham Lincoln and sang for 75,000 people. The same year she was awarded the Spingarn Medal.

Four years later, in 1943, Marian married Orpheus Fisher, whom she had known for a long time. Mr. Fisher was an architect. He designed the home that they built in Danbury, Connecticut, which they called Marrianna Farm.

In 1955, after thirty years as a successful concert singer, Marian appeared with the world-famous Metropolitan Opera Company in New York. She took the part of Ulrica, the Gypsy fortune-teller, in Verdi's opera *The Masked Ball*. It was the first time an African-American had sung an important role at the Metropolitan as a regular company member. Marian had opened a door for her own people. From this time on, African-American singers were welcome on the great opera stage.

Marian was growing older, so in 1956 she made a farewell tour of Europe and America. As she took her last bows from the stage, she thought, "My work is not over. There is still much I can do. I want to help people of different groups come to understand each other. I can make the way easier for young singers. I want to do something for children all over the world—with my hands, and my heart, and my soul. In a way, my work is just beginning."

Marian received many honors. In 1957 she toured twelve Asian nations at the request of the U.S. State Department. She sang to the people and talked with them. They shared some of their deep thoughts with her about their needs and hopes for their country. In September of 1958, Marian was named to the U.S. delegation to the United Nations in New York City. She was sent to the United Nations with leaders of many countries to try to bring peace to the world. By that time, her autobiography, *My Lord, What a Morning*, had been published.

In 1982, when Marian celebrated her eightieth birthday, Grace Bumbry and Shirley Verrett sang at New York City's Carnegie Hall in tribute to Marian. Ms. Verrett hailed Ms. Anderson as "a dream maker." Ms. Verrett and Ms. Bumbry are both former recipients of Marian Anderson's scholarships.

In 1986, Marian received the National Medal of Arts. She made one of her rare public appearances in her home state, Pennsylvania, in January 1991 at the dedication of St. Christopher's Hospital for Children's new pediatric sickle-cell anemia clinic and research center, named in her honor. Marian died at age ninety-one at the home of her nephew in Portland, Oregon.

Educator

Mary McLeod Bethune

MARY McLEOD BETHUNE
(Born 1875—Died 1955)

Mary McLeod Bethune was the first African-American woman to head a federal office. She set up an Office of Minority Affairs in the informal African Cabinet of the New Deal. During the 1930s, she was one of the leading figures and the only African-American woman in the unofficial "Black Cabinet," which had begun the fight for advanced integration in the U.S. government.

Mrs. Bethune has often been compared to Frederick Douglass for, like him, she overcame tremendous obstacles to rise to prominence. While Douglass, the former slave, became an internationally famous author, speaker, and fighter for human rights, Mrs. Bethune, once a field hand, became a college president and Spingarn Medal winner.

Mary Jane McLeod was born in a log cabin near Mayesville, South Carolina, on July 10, 1875. This is where she gained her special insight into the everyday problems of the average African-American. Her father and mother had once been slaves. Mary had fourteen older brothers and sisters. She was the fifteenth child and two others were born later.

Every morning, Mary's mother and father and her brothers and sisters would go to the fields to work on the farm that belonged to them. They grew vegetables and rice to eat and cotton to sell. It was hard work, but the McLeods were thankful for their freedom.

After the McLeods had paid for their small farm and built the cabin, there was no money left for tables and chairs. Except for Mary's grandmother's rocker, all the furniture was made

23

from boards her father got at the lumber mill. Her mother stuffed sacks with corn shucks and straw to make beds. Her father built shelves near the fireplace for pots and pans and her mother cooked over the open fire. The Bible was kept on a special shelf in the cabin. The family treasured it, even though no one could read it.

As Mary worked in the fields, she used part of her mind to think about her favorite dream. She thought about one day being able to read, and about having her own books and going to school. There were no schools near Mayesville for African-American children.

Sometimes Mary's mother would wash clothes for white people in town. One day, when Mary was seven, she helped her mother carry the clean wash back to the Wilson house. While Mary's mother took the clothes inside, Mary played with the Wilson girls. Mary saw an open storybook on the table and she asked the girls to tell her what the words said. The oldest girl frowned, snatched the book away, and told Mary that her father said that "Negroes can't learn to read." Mary was hurt and sad and she asked her mother why she couldn't learn to read. Her mother told her she could because she was just as smart as the Wilson girls or anybody, but there were no schools for poor African-American folks like them. Still Mary dreamed of learning to read.

Every morning and evening Mary's family stood in front of the fireplace and said prayers and sang hymns together. After dinner, the children gathered around their grandmother as she sat in her favorite chair and told them true stories about Africa and talked about the Bible. Listening to the stories made Mary want to read even more. She talked about reading all the time.

One day when Mary was eleven years old, Ms. Emma Wilson, an African-American teacher, was sent by a Presbyterian church to Mayesville to start a one-room school for African-American children. Mary's parents wanted all of their children to go to school, but there was too much work to be done on the farm. Only one could go, and they decided that one would be Mary.

Mary was happy to walk all the miles to the little school by the railroad tracks, because every step was taking her closer to something that she had wanted for a long, long time. The school had only backless benches, a stove, and a desk and chair for the teacher. There were few books and no paper and pencils. Children used slates and chalk to write their first lessons.

Ms. Wilson was a good teacher and Mary was a good student. She studied hard every day and soon she could read short words and work arithmetic problems. In the evening, she taught her family what she had learned in school. Sometimes neighbors would ask her to read their mail for them, figure out how much money they should get for selling their cotton, or add up their grocery bills so the storekeeper could not charge them too much.

In the fall there was a new brick schoolhouse. The Mission Board had sent more books, paper, and pencils. A few years later, Mary had learned all Ms. Wilson could teach so she was graduated from the school. Mary Crissman, a dressmaker from Denver, had sent money to educate an African-American girl and the Mission Board chose Mary McLeod for the scholarship. At no charge, Mary was able to enroll at Scotia Seminary, a school for African-American girls in Concord, North Carolina.

Mary was nervous about leaving her family for the first time and taking her first train ride, but she was excited, too. Her mother made a dress for her out of a piece of cloth that was pretty, although it wasn't new. When her friends and neighbors heard the good news they knitted collars and shawls as gifts. They made some of their dresses over to fit Mary. Even the storekeeper sold her shoes at a lesser price.

Many things at Scotia Seminary were new to Mary. She slept on a real bed for the the first time and she learn to use a fork because at home they had always eaten with spoons. All the students at Scotia helped with the housework. Mary dusted, ironed, and brought in coal for the fire. Much of her free time was spent in the library reading about Africa.

Seven years later Mary McLeod graduated from Scotia. She

received another scholarship—this time to study at the Moody Bible Institute in Chicago, where she would study to be a missionary. Mary believed in the Christian religion and wanted other people to believe in it, too. She knew the people in Africa and other parts of the world had their own religion, but Mary wanted to go to Africa to teach Christianity.

While at Moody, Mary and other students were sent out to visit prisoners in the jail and people who were sick or without money. The students read the Bible to them, prayed, and sang hymns. They also helped other people whenever they could and invited them to come to the school for church services. Mary and five other students traveled to other states to start Sunday schools. They rode in a train "The Gospel Car."

When Mary finished her work at Moody, she had grown up. She was a woman now, rather large, with smooth, dark skin. She had learned all that Moody could teach and was ready to be a missionary. But she was very unhappy to find that there were no openings for an African-American missionary in Africa.

When this course proved impossible, Mary decided to become a teacher. She was happy to return home to Mayesville, because during the years that she was away she had not been able to visit her family. But she was disappointed to have to go back home without the job she had studied so hard for. She helped Ms. Wilson in Mayesville School until she got a job as a teacher at Haines Institute in Augusta, Georgia.

Haines Institute had been started by Lucy Laney, who had once been a slave. Ms. Laney was still in charge of the school. She never seemed to get tired of helping her students and the teachers who worked for her. She always had new ideas to make Haines better. Watching her, Mary soon forgot her disappointment and put all of herself into being the best teacher she could be. Mary realized that there were African-American children in her own country who needed her help. At Haines, Mary trained a chorus, teaching the songs she had learned from her grandmother, Sophia. Rich visitors would come to Augusta in the winter to hear the chorus and they would give money to help the school.

26

Most of what Mary earned she sent home to her family so she could help pay for the education of her younger sisters. She also bought her parents a new home, because their old one had burned down. Next she was sent to teach at Kendall Institute in Sumter, South Carolina. It was only a few miles from her home. There she met another teacher, Albertus Bethune, whom she married. They moved to Savannah, and the next year their son was born.

While Mrs. Bethune took care of her baby she thought about her dream, about Ms. Laney and Ms. Wilson, and she remembered herself as a child longing to learn. There were many African-American children like herself who lived in places without schools, who had questions but no answers, who wanted to learn, and she wanted to teach them.

Mrs. Bethune heard about Daytona Beach, Florida, where the new East Coast Railroad was being built. African-American men had come to help build it, while others worked in the turpentine mills. There were no schools for the workers' children, so Mrs. Bethune felt she must do something about it. A short time later the Bethunes moved to Palatka, Florida. With little Albert in her arms and only $1.50, Mrs. Bethune begged a ride to Daytona Beach. She stayed with a friend, and every day she went for a walk, looking for a building that she could use as a school. Finally, she found an empty two-story cottage on the beach and rented it on credit. The owner agreed to wait a few weeks for the rent, which was $11 a month.

Mrs. Bethune visited the homes of African-American families, telling them about her school. Neighbors came to paint the cottage and fix the broken steps and the children helped with the cleaning. The school opened on an autumn day in 1904, with five little girls.

The school was named the Normal and Industrial School for Girls. There was no furniture and little food. Mrs. Bethune and the girls found boxes and boards on a nearby trash pile. They made benches and tables and a neighbor gave them a stove. They burned logs and used the charcoal as pencils, and they mashed berries and used the juice as ink.

The children loved the school. Some of them lived there with Mrs. Bethune and all of them wanted to help raise money for the rent, books, paper, lamps, and beds that they needed. After school was over, the children and Mrs. Bethune made ice cream and pies to sell to the tourists. Mrs. Bethune and the children gave programs at hotels and in churches where the children sang and recited and Mrs. Bethune spoke to the audiences about the school.

News spread that Mary Bethune had opened a school for African-American girls. More students came, but only a few could pay. Mrs. Bethune trained a chorus and the Florida tourists enjoyed the music. They came to visit the school and gave money for a better building, new furniture, and more books.

Mary Bethune kept busy with her school all the time. Soon her husband began to say it was a waste of time. After a few years he went back to South Carolina.

Before long the school had 250 students. It was moved to a larger campus and better buildings were built. Mrs. Bethune named the new main building Faith Hall in honor of her favorite building at Scotia Seminary. She had faith in God, in herself, and in African-American people. Over the door she hung a sign that said, *Enter to Learn*. Now there were many teachers and Mrs. Bethune wrote hundreds of letters to rich people asking help for her school. It was called Bethune College.

Over the years Mary Bethune fought many hard battles for the rights of her people. One day, a student became very ill. Because there were no hospitals for African-Americans for many, many miles, Mrs. Bethune rushed her to the nearest white hospital. The doctor agreed to take care of her, but when Mrs. Bethune went back to the hospital to see the student, she found her on a cot on the back porch. Mrs. Bethune was very angry. After that she rented another house and started a two-bed hospital for African-American people. She named it McLeod Hospital in memory of her deceased father. It saved many African-American lives.

Mrs. Bethune's school, which started as an elementary

school for girls, became a high school, then a junior college, and was given a new name when it merged in 1923 with a men's college. The new name of the college became Bethune-Cookman College, with Mrs. Bethune as president. It had the only library for African-American people in that part of Florida. The chorus still sang in many cities to raise money. Mrs. Bethune served as president of the college until 1947.

Mrs. Bethune did not spend all of her time at the school. She joined groups of people who were working for the rights of African-American men, women, and children. She wrote articles for newspapers and magazines. She traveled across the United States making speeches about the need for public schools, jobs, houses, and food. She became famous for her devotion to African-American youths.

In 1930 President Hoover invited Mrs. Bethune to the White House. She spoke on African-American rights at a conference on child health and protection. In 1936 President Franklin D. Roosevelt asked her to work in the National Youth Association (NYA). The new job meant that she would have to live in Washington, D.C. She did not want to leave her school, but she knew that she was needed for this special job. So she moved to Washington and worked to find jobs for young African-Americans all over the country. She visited many states and talked to these young people about their problems.

After a year on the job, Mrs. Bethune's work so impressed the president that he was persuaded to set up an Office of Minority Affairs, with Mrs. Bethune as administrator. This established a precedent, for it was the first post of its kind ever to be held by an African-American woman.

Congressional appropriations for the NYA continued from 1936 through 1944, and Mrs. Bethune's title was soon changed to the more specific one of director of the Division of Negro Affairs. Her duties consisted largely of granting funds to deserving students, particularly African-American, who could not otherwise have continued graduate study.

Mrs. Bethune also participated in antidiscrimination protests. When Executive Order 8802 on the Fair Employment

29

Practices Commission (issued by President Roosevelt after A. Philip Randolph's threat of a mass march on Washington) was not enforced, Mrs. Bethune was one of the African-Americans who spoke at a Madison Square Garden protest rally in 1942.

Mrs. Bethune was heartbroken when President Roosevelt died suddenly. Later, his wife, Eleanor, gave Mrs. Bethune the president's walking cane, which she carried with her as she grew older.

As the years passed, Mrs. Bethune was given many awards for her good work. Ten colleges gave her honorary degrees. She was president of the National Association of Colored Women's Club (1924-28), and she was founder of the National Association of Colored Women (1926) and founder-president of the National Council of Negro Women (1935-49). Mrs. Bethune was also a member of the Hoover Committee for Child Welfare and director of the National Business League, the National Urban League, and the Commission of Interracial Cooperation.

At the age of seventy, Mrs. Bethune served as advisor to President Truman, and was an observer at the initial meeting of the United Nations in San Francisco. Her philosophy was epitomized in a phrase she often used in lecturing African-American audiences: "This is our day!"

After many years, Mrs. Bethune returned to her home on the campus of Bethune-Cookman College. She kept working, doing more and more for her countrymen and all the people of the world. She went to Liberia in Africa and to Switzerland to meet and talk with people. Mrs. Bethune always traveled around the United States, speaking about and working for the rights of African-American people, for more freedom for women, and for better education for everyone.

Mrs. Bethune spent her life working to help others. She was president of the Association for the Study of Negro Life and History, working with Dr. Carter G. Woodson to make known the true history of African-American people. In 1949 Mrs. Bethune was one of the main speakers at the annual meeting of the National Council of Negro Women. Her speech was heard on the radio all over the country.

Mrs. Bethune eventually had to stop working, because she was sick more often with asthma and her heart was weak. But still she kept assisting others and giving advice when needed.

In 1955, at the age of eighty, Mary McLeod Bethune died of a heart attack. She was buried on the grounds of Bethune-Cookman College. In her will, she left a message for African-American people. She said that they must believe in themselves and help each other; she said that it is through learning that children grow up to be strong men and women and that children must never stop wanting to build a better world.

Nineteen years after Mrs. Bethune's death, a statue was erected in her honor in Washington, D.C. Some of the words from her will are written on the base of the statue: *I leave you faith, I leave you hope, I leave you love.*

MARY MCLEOD BETHUNE'S LEGACY

I LEAVE YOU LOVE. Love builds. It is positive and hopeful. It is more beneficial than hate . . . Personally and racially, our emenies must be forgiven . . . "Love thy neighbor" is a precept which would transform the world if it were universally practiced. Loving your neighbor means being interracial, interreligious, and international.

I LEAVE YOU HOPE. Yesterday, our ancestors endured the degradulation of slavery, yet they retained their dignity. Today, we direct our economic and political strength toward winning a more abundant and secure life. Tomorrow, a new Negro, unhindered by race taboos and shackles, will benefit from more than 330 years of ceaseless striving and struggle. Theirs will be a better world. This I believe with all my heart.

I LEAVE YOU A THRIST FOR EDUCATION. Knowledge is the prime need of the hour. More and more, Negroes are taking full advantages of hard-won opportunities for learning, and the educational level of the Negro population is at its highest point in history . . . If we continue in this trend, we will be able to rear increasing numbers of strong purposeful men and women, equipped with vision, mental clarity, health, and education.

I LEAVE YOU THE CHALLENGE OF DEVELOPING CONFIDENCE IN ONE ANOTHER. As long as Negroes are hemmed into racial blocs of prejudice and pressure, it will be necessary for them to band together for economic betterment. Negro banks, insurance companies, and other businesses are examples of successful racial economic enterprises. These institutions were made possible by vision and mutual aid. Confidence was vital in getting them going. Negroes have got to demonstrate still more confidence in each other in business . . . We must spread out as far as we can, but we must also help each other as we go.

I LEAVE YOU A RESPECT FOR THE USE OF POWER. We live in a world which respects power above all things. Power, intelligently directed, can lead to more freedom. Unwisely directed, it can be a dreadful destructive force. During my lifetime I have seen the power of the Negro grow enormously. We must select leaders who are wise and courageous, and of great moral stature and ability. We have great leaders among us today. We have had other great men and women in the past: Frederick Douglass, Booker T. Washington, Harriet Tubman, Sojourner Truth, and Mary Church Terrell. We must produce more qualified people like them, who will work not for themselves, but for others.

I LEAVE YOU FAITH. Without faith nothing is possible. With it, nothing is impossible. Faith in God is the greatest power, but great too is faith in oneself. In 50 years the faith of the American Negro in himself has grown immensely, and is still increasing. The measure of our progress as a race is in precise relation to the depth of faith in our people held by our leaders. Frederick Douglass . . . was spurred by a deep conviction that his people would heed his counsel and follow him to freedom. Our greatest Negro figures have been imbued with faith . . . We must never forget their sufferings and their sacrifices, for they were the foundations of the progress of our people.

I LEAVE YOU RACIAL DIGNITY. I want Negroes to maintain their human dignity at all cost. We, as Negroes, must recognize that we are the custodians as well as the heirs of a great civilization. We have given something to the world as a race and for this we are proud and fully conscious of our place in the total picture of mankind's development. We must learn also to share and mix with all men . . .

I LEAVE YOU A DESIRE TO LIVE HARMONIOUSLY WITH YOUR FELLOW MAN. The problem of color is world-wide. It is found in Africa and Asia, Europe and South America. I appeal to American Negroes—both North and South, East and West—to recognize their common problems and unite to solve them. I pray that we will begin to live harmoniously with the white race . . . We are a minority of fifteen millions living side by side with a white majority. We must learn to deal with people positively and on an individual basis.

I LEAVE YOU, FINALLY, A RESPONSIBILITY TO OUR YOUNG PEOPLE. The world around us really belongs to youth, for youth will take over its future management. Our children must never lose their zeal for building a better world. They must not be discouraged from aspiring toward greatness, for they are to be the leaders of tomorrow. Nor must they forget that the masses of our people are still underprivileged, ill-housed, improverished, and victimized by discrimination. We have a powerful potential in our youth, and we must have the courage to change old ideas and practices so that we may direct their power toward good ends.

FAITH, COURAGE, BROTHERHOOD, DIGNITY, AMBITION, RESPONSBILITY— these are needed today as never before. We must cultivate them and use them as tools for our task of completing the establishment of equality for the Negro. We must sharpen these tools in the struggle that faces us and find new ways of using them. The Freedom Gates are half ajar. We must pry them fully open.

IF I HAVE A LEGACY TO LEAVE MY PEOPLE, it is my philosophy of living and serving. As I face tomorrow, I am content, for I think I have spent my life well. I pray now that my philosophy may be helpful to those who share my vision of a world of peace.

Poet

Gwendolyn Brooks

GWENDOLYN BROOKS
(Born 1917—Died 2000)

Poet Gwendolyn Brooks was the first African-American to win a Pulitzer Prize. She was born in Topeka, Kansas on June 7, 1917. Ms. Brooks moved to Chicago at an early age, was educated at Englewood High School, and graduated from Wilson Junior College in 1936.

Ms. Brooks later enrolled in a poetry class at the South Side Community Art Center and in 1943 she won her first prize in poetry and a new African-American Experience began. Much of her work focuses on the conflict between the individual African-American and the African-American community. Ms. Brooks taught at many Chicago schools, sometimes at as many as three at a time. She taught creative writing at Columbia College in Chicago, Northwestern Illinois State College, City University in New York, and the University of Wisconsin.

Ms. Brooks had her first taste of the more sordid aspects of ghetto life during her first job as secretary to a "spiritual advisor" who sold "love drops" or illegal drugs. Although unfamiliar with these conditions, she nonetheless realized that they could offer her much in the way of unique material for her writing.

In 1945, she completed a book of poems, *A Street in Bronzeville,* and was selected by *Mademoiselle* as one of the year's ten most outstanding American women. She received the American Academy of Arts and Letters award for creative writing in 1946 and Guggenheim Fellowships for 1946 and 1947.

In 1949 she won the Eunice Tietjen Prize for Poetry in the annual competition sponsored by *Poetry* magazine. Her

Pulitzer Prize was awarded in 1950 for her volume of poetry entitled *Annie Allen*. She was poet laureate of the state of Illinois in 1969 and was named a consultant on literature to the Library of Congress in 1973. Ms. Brooks has been credited with starting a trend in poetry of going back to the issues and problems of urban life and away from academic detachment. Her work, like that of the late Langston Hughes, has always touched at some level on the problems of African-Americans in America. Ms. Brooks was often singled out as the "exception" and proclaimed as an "artist," a poet of first rank.

Her other books include a novel, *Maud Martha* (1953); a collection of children's poems, *Bronzeville Boys and Girls* (1956); and two books of poetry, *The Bean Eaters* (1960) and *Selected Poems* (1963). She has also written *In the Mecca* (for which she received the Anisfield-Wolf Award in 1968), *Riot, The World of Gwendolyn Brooks, Report from Part One: An Autobiography, Family Pictures, Beckonings, Aloneness, Primer for Blacks*, and *To Disembark*.

Ms. Brooks' poems and stories have also been published in magazines and the anthologies *Soon, One Morning*, and *Beyond the Angry Black*. She has edited *A Broadside Treasury, Jump Bad*, and *A New Chicago Anthology*.

Overall, Ms. Brooks' body of work has done more than bring her personal fame. It has placed her in a position to help other poets. For years, until her travel schedule became too busy, her home was all but an open poetry workshop. Many young African-American poets were able to hone their skills under her direction.

Annie Allen (1949)

What shall I give my children? who are poor,
Who are adjudged the leastwise of the land.

"Beckonings" (1975)

Beware the easy griefs
that fool and fuel nothing.

Actress

Diahann Carroll

DIAHANN CARROLL
(Born 1935—   )

Diahann Carroll was the first African-American to star in a long-running network television series. Aside from appearing in "Julia," she has had a career in films, on stage, in nightclubs, and in the recording industry.

Ms. Carroll was born in the Bronx, the daughter of a subway conductor and a nurse. Her family moved to Harlem, but when Diahann was one and a half years old she was sent to North Carolina to live with her mother's sister for a few years. Both of her parents had to work, so this arrangement was to help them get on their feet.

This experience caused Diahann a lot of problems when she grew up, because she was plagued by such terrible feelings of insecurity and rejections in relationships. When a man would tell her he loved her she didn't believe it and always insisted that he keep proving it over and over again. Finally, at age twenty-eight, during one of her therapy sessions, her mind went back to her childhood, when she lived at her aunt's home without her parents. She saw why she wanted to be good so that no one would leave her, why she wanted to make those who loved her prove it, and why she wanted to be led by those who cared for her.

Ms. Carroll felt that her life was very complicated. The feelings surrounding her were so often contradictory. She was adored, catered to, and given as many advantages as her parents could have possibly given a child, yet she often felt estranged. Her parents tried to protect her from the cruelties of white racism. Ms. Carroll felt proud to be an African-

American, but the culture she saw in magazines and movies, the people her parents held up as successful, were white. Because of this she was very stubborn in her conviction that, no matter the circumstances, she would hold her head up. This made her relentless in her ambition to stand out in the crowd—to be somebody whom people notice and respect. She was determined to sing.

Ms. Carroll had begun singing in public when she was ten years old and back in New York, as part of the "Tiny Tot" choir in Dr. Adam Clayton Powell's Abyssinian Baptist Church. A few years later she started taking lessons in downtown Manhattan. She auditioned and won a scholarship from an organization affiliated with the Manhattan Opera.

Ms. Carroll's experience at Still Junior High School was not happy. Her guidance counselor suggested that she attend the George Washington High School of Music and Art. Around this time her sister Lydia was born and she adored her.

When she was seventeen, Diahann took her first modeling job, for Johnson Publications. She worked as a model for *Ebony* too, but since music and art were demanding, she could not work very often. It was after she appeared on Arthur Godfrey's "Talent Scouts" that Carol Diann Johnson's name was changed to Diahann Carroll.

When she graduated from high school Diahann went to New York University to study psychology. She tried to be a good student for her parents. Early in her freshman year she entered another talent contest, a network TV show called "Chance of a Lifetime," where she sang "Why Was I Born?" "The Man I Love," and "Someone to Watch Over Me." She won for three weeks in a row. Her prize was $3,000 and a week's engagement at the Latin Quarter. With her modeling, rehearsals, voice lessons, and singing jobs, she didn't have much time for school. Her parents agreed to give her two years to establish her career. If that didn't happen, she would go back to New York University and finish her degree.

In that same year, 1954, Ms. Carroll appeared in her first

Broadway play, *House of Flowers,* winning favorable press notices as a refreshing personality, "with a rich, lovely, easy voice." Composer Richard Rodgers encountered her for the first time during the play, and resolved on the spot to write a show for her someday.

In September 1956 Ms. Carroll married Monte Kay, whose real name was Fremont Kaplan. Dr. Adam Clayton Powell performed the ceremony. Monte and Diahann had a daughter, Suzanne.

Movies and television appearances kept Ms. Carroll busy until 1958, the year she was slated to appear as an Oriental in Rodgers' *Flower Drum Song.* The part did not materialize, however, largely due to Ms. Carroll's height and makeup problems.

Rodgers asked her about the kind of role she would like to perform on Broadway. The result of the exchange was a subsequent commitment by Rodgers to cast her as a high-fashion model playing opposite a hesitant and troubled Pulitzer-Prize-winning author. The show was not a smashing success, although elements of it, including Ms. Carroll's performance, received good notices. *The New York Times* critic, Howard Taubman, singled out her special talent for putting across the show's rich melodies, alluding to her ability to create and sustain a sense of involvement. "You must be able . . . to make the audience feel," Ms. Caroll says, "that the words have meaning to the singer—that you are not just repeating them, but that they come from your very being."

In September 1968 Ms. Carroll starred in the television series "Julia" on NBC, the first African-American to star in a television program. The success of the program was remarkable. Many African-Americans criticized the program because it did not include an African-American father. In this series Ms. Caroll was cast as a nurse and war widow.

Ms. Carroll won a Tony for her performance in the Broadway production *No Strings.* Some of her films included *Porgy and Bess, Goodbye Again, Paris Blue,* and in 1974, *Claudine* with James Earl Jones, a serious comedy in which she played a mother struggling to raise children in Harlem, a role for which she was nominated for an Academy Award.

Following the death of her husband in 1981, she was making only occasional appearances. In 1984, she joined the cast of the television nighttime series "Dynasty," playing the part of Dominique Deveraux.

U.S. Representative

Shirley Chisholm

SHIRLEY CHISHOLM
(Born 1924—   )

Shirley Chisholm was the first African-American woman ever elected to Congress and the first African-American woman to serve on the powerful House Rules Committee. She was also the first African-American woman to run in the New York Democratic primary for president of the United States.

Shirley was born in Brooklyn, New York on November 30, 1924 as Shirley Anita St. Hill. She is descended from West Indian immigrant laborers; her mother was a seamstress from Barbados and her father, a native of British Guiana in South America (now called Guyana), worked in a burlap factory. At the age of three, Shirley and her two sisters and four cousins went to Barbados to stay with their grandmother (Emmeline Seales). Their parents were working hard in Brooklyn to save their money for the girls' education, so that one day the family could be together again. Shirley grew up in Barbados as a plump little girl because there was always so much food to eat.

Shirley attended a school in the village of Vanxhall from nine o'clock in the morning to four o'clock in the afternoon. She used slates and chalk instead of paper and pencil, an old British custom that, like many others, lingered on the island of Barbados long after dying out in Britain. Shirley learned to read at the age of four and by five she was able to copy the alphabet neatly onto her slate. By the age of six Shirley was the brightest one among her sisters and cousins. In the classroom Shirley began to listen in on the older children's lessons, with the teacher's approval.

During the week Shirley's routine was school, chores, and

homework. On Sundays everybody on her grandmother's farm got up early, and two at a time, the children got a good scrubbing in the wooden tub in the backyard and then put on their freshly ironed Sunday clothes. Shirley and her sisters wore starched pink and yellow dresses with little round collars. Her boy cousins and uncle wore dark suits and black shoes and her grandmother dressed in black. After breakfast they walked two miles to church. It was not unusual for Shirley and her family to go to church three or four times on Sunday.

When Shirley was ten years old her mother returned to Barbados to carry her and her sisters back to Brooklyn. The trip home would not be simple. For two weeks Shirley's mother and aunt made several trips to Bridgetown, the capital of Barbados, where they were thoroughly examined by a doctor who had to fill out forms stating that the children were in good health and did not have a disease like mumps, measles, or chicken pox. The smaller children had to be vaccinated. The boat took six days to reach New York. This ended the carefree, sunny part of Shirley's childhood.

Her parents lived in an apartment in the Brownsville section of Brooklyn on Liberty Avenue. The apartment did have hot water, but there was no central heating. By this time Shirley and her sisters were used to the tropical sun of Barbados. Now they were miserable and one after the other they each caught a cold. It took some time for Shirley to adjust to Brooklyn and the city streets. She had never seen so much traffic: cars, buses, and trucks.

Shirley and her sisters developed a love for dance. Their mother felt if they liked music that much she would purchase a secondhand piano. Shirley spent many pleasant hours practicing, but this did not stop her from dancing. She won several prizes at local dance competitions, and to her, winning was a good feeling. But she never let these dance prizes turn her away from her first love, reading. The three women Shirley admired were Harriet Tubman, Susan B. Anthony, and Mary McLeod Bethune.

When Shirley graduated from high school she received four

scholarships to different colleges, but she decided to take the one to Brooklyn College because the others would only pay for her tuition. If she went to Brooklyn she could live at home free and the scholarship would pay for her books and supplies. Shirley decided to major in sociology, so she could learn how different groups of people behave among themselves and how they relate to society. She always had an interest in the relationship between African-Americans and whites and between the rich and the poor in Brooklyn. She wanted to be a social worker. Shirley was sure that whatever she did it would have something to do with helping others, and sociology would help her to understand a lot about the world.

It was in college that Shirley realized that she loved to argue a political point. She was never shy about speaking up in school, despite the difficulty she had in pronouncing the letter *s*. The Debating Society became her favorite after-class club. Shirley discovered she was turning into a fiery speaker who could stand up on her two feet and talk with just a page of notes and facts to guide her. She loved being the captain and "cleanup" speaker for her team, the one who summed up all their facts. She realized that she could persuade people when she spoke and that she was getting better at it all the time. It made her feel good to be able to move people with words and to convince them with facts and a clearly presented argument.

In Shirley's senior year in college, Professor Warsoff called her into his office and asked her if she had thought about what she was going to do after graduation. Shirley told him that she would like to help other children the way she was helped to learn to read and write. The professor asked her if she would find the teaching profession challenging enough. He stated that she was a young woman with a lot of energy and a very scrappy personality, and she was obviously quite concerned with social issues. He wondered if she had ever thought of going into politics.

Shirley was shocked, because the only African-American woman she had ever heard of in politics was Mary McLeod Bethune, and she wasn't really in politics, but was an educator

47

to whom President Roosevelt gave important government assignments. Then she asked him how many African-American women did he know of in politics and in the United States Congress? The professor told her none, but there's got to be a first sometime, and he felt that she was the right person.

Shirley was speechless, because she seldom confided her hopes and ambitions to anyone, and here was this white man, a college professor, who was talking to her about her future and describing goals far greater than those she usually allowed herself to dream about. He told Shirley that he was not suggesting that she go out tomorrow and run for Congress, but that she get involved on a local level in her community, help people with their problems, and try to correct some of the wrongs. He told her the first step is to recognize the problems and the second step is to begin to do something about them. Professor Warsoff told Shirley to apply her mind, energy, and gift of speech to organize neighborhood people who are willing to fight to change conditions. He explained to Shirley what politics was all about.

Shirley graduated from Brooklyn College in 1946. The war had been over one year and her father had managed to save enough money to put down on a nice three-story, brick row house on Prospect Place at the edge of Bedford-Stuyvesant. Finally her parents were homeowners in Brooklyn. Shirley's first job was as a nursery-school teacher at the Mount Calvary Child Care Center. After work she took evening classes at the Columbia School of Education, working for a master's degree. The schedule Shirley set for herself, rushing from job to school and then back home again to sleep, was a rugged one. It left her no time for a social life. She planned her weekends so she could devote most of her time to studying. Because she still loved to dance, she would take time to go dancing.

At one of those rare Saturday night dances, Shirley was introduced by friends to a graduate student from Jamaica named Conrad Chisholm. A year later the two were married. Shirley was twenty-five years old and had completed her master's. Later she was appointed director of a private nursery

48

school in Brownsville. Her husband understood that Shirley's career was important to her and he always encouraged her to do her best. Conrad and Shirley promised each other that they would never interfere with each other's career and would always help each other to the best of their ability.

Mrs. Chisholm was later appointed director of the Hamilton-Madison Child Care Center on the Lower East Side of Manhattan, in the middle of a huge housing project. She started her political career when she volunteered to work in the campaign of Lewis Flagg at the Bedford-Stuyvesant Political League. Her candidate lost, but she joined the Unity Club and helped campaign for Tom Jones. He won. During his term in the State Assembly, Tom Jones would come back and give progress reports to the members of the Unity Club. Mrs. Chisholm became very fascinated by his description of the political process. She wished she could be the one who introduced bills and tried to steer them through their various stages all the way up to the governor.

Mrs. Chisholm was appointed New York City's chief educational consultant for all of its day nurseries and she spent her working days traveling from day-care center to day-care center, giving advice to the center's directors and straightening out problems whenever they arose. At this time, the members of the Unity Club elected Mrs. Chisholm as co-leader. In 1964 Assemblyman Jones was up for reelection but he had been asked to be the candidate for civil court judge and he agreed. The Unity Club chose Shirley Chisholm to be their candidate for the State Assembly. She went on to win the Democratic primary and the general election as well. In 1964 she became the first African-American woman to be elected to public office in Brooklyn.

Mrs. Chisholm served four years in Albany and had nine bills of her own passed by the assembly. Her first proud accomplishment was a bill to extend unemployment insurance coverage to domestic workers. The Democratic leaders in the assembly assigned her to the Committee on Education because of her teaching background. She was able to get her fellow

49

assemblymen to support the SEEK bill, "Search for Education, Elevation, and Knowledge," which gave funds to African-
American and Puerto Rican youths who showed that they have
the potential to go to college.

In 1968 Mrs. Chisholm announced her candidacy for
Brooklyn's new Twelfth Congressional District. Her first job
was to win the Democratic primary. Two weeks before the New
York primary, Sen. Robert Kennedy was assassinated, which
was two months after the assassination of Dr. Martin Luther
King, Jr. It was a bad time for the country but Mrs. Chisholm
won the Democratic nomination for Congress.

Half of her battle was won. Now she needed to win the
general election in November. The National Democratic Convention was held in Chicago at the end of August and Mrs.
Chisholm was elected as national committeewoman from the
state of New York. On November 5, 1968 Shirley Chisholm
won the race for Congress. This was a great honor, because she
was the nation's first African-American congresswoman. Also
that year, Louis Stokes from Missouri became the first African-
American man of his state to join the House of Representatives, bringing the number of African-American representatives in Congress to nine.

After Mrs. Chisholm's election to Congress, she indicated
her preference for committee assignments that would reflect
her interests and areas of expertise (education, labor management, and inner-city conditions in general) and that would
take advantage of her experience in the social sciences. When
saddled with a committee assignment in the area of agricul-
ture, she not only openly resisted the idea, but complained
outspokenly of the gross misuse of her talents. Other committees in which she expressed interest were the Foreign Relations
Committee, due to her concern for U.S. policy with Africa,
and the Postal and Civil Service Committee. She believed that
African-Americans made an unusually high human invest-
ment in postal and civil service work without reaping some of
the more obvious rewards available to those who climb into
upper-level management.

In 1969 Mrs. Chisholm was initiated into Delta Sigma Theta Sorority, Inc., an organization of African-American college graduates and professional women.

On January 25, 1972, Congresswoman Chisholm leaped to national prominence when she announced her candidacy for the Democratic nomination for the president of the United States. She entered a larger number of primaries and though her share of the vote never exceeded 7 percent, she was regarded with the same respect as the white male candidates. Mrs. Chisholm received only some 150 of 1,600 delegate votes at the Miami Convention, as a great many African-Americans supported Sen. George McGovern or Sen. Hubert Humphrey rather than her. She had been the target of considerable criticism from African-American leaders and her constituents for her avid support of women's liberation. She was quoted as saying that "discrimination against women exceeds discrimination against African-Americans." Many African-Americans who agreed with the objectives of "women's lib" felt that such views diverted attention from the needs of African-Americans, men and women alike.

However, Shirley Chisholm was a well-liked figure among her constituents and she continued to win her seat in each election by large margins. Just before the beginning of her second term in office she published her autobiography, entitled *Unbought and Unbossed.*

Shirley Chisholm was divorced in 1977 from her first husband, Conrad Chisholm. That same year she married Arthur Hardwick, an architectural designer whom she met thirteen years earlier when they both served in the New York State Assembly.

Shirley surprised many people in 1982 when she announced that after serving seven full terms in Congress she would not seek another term. She wanted to return to "a more private life."

51

Tennis Champion

Althea Gibson

ALTHEA GIBSON
(Born 1927—   )

Althea Gibson was the first African-American woman to play at Wimbledon. In 1957 she won the Wimbledon singles crown, and teamed with Darlene Hard to win the doubles championship as well. When she returned to New York, she was greeted by a ticker-tape parade in recognition of her position as the best woman tennis player in the world.

Althea was born in Silver, South Carolina on August 25, 1927 and was raised in Harlem. As a child, she played almost every sport imaginable: basketball, shuffleboard, volleyball, and paddle tennis. After she graduated from junior high school in 1941 she attended Yorkville Trade School. Eventually she dropped out of school and started working.

Meanwhile, Althea had discovered tennis. She started with paddle tennis, a game played with wooden bats, or paddles, and a sponge ball on a court much like a tennis court but about half the size. Paddle tennis was one of the games played on the block where Althea lived, 143rd Street. It was a Police Athletic League play street, which meant that it was closed to traffic during the daytime for use as a playground. Althea played here and attracted the attention of Buddy Walker, a musician who supplemented his income by working for the city during the summer months as a playground leader. Recognizing her potential, Buddy talked Althea into trying her hand at tennis. He started her off hitting balls against a wall in Morris Park with a secondhand tennis racket he bought her.

Having taught her the rudiments of the game, Buddy took Althea to the Harlem River Tennis Court at 150th Street and Seventh Avenue to play with some of his friends. Althea ran

55

their legs off. Players on other courts stopped their games to watch her play. She was a phenomenon. One of the spectators, Juan Serrell, a young schoolteacher who was a member of the Cosmopolitan Tennis Club, saw that Althea was tournament material. He insisted that she be taken to the Cosmopolitan, where she could get expert instruction from Fred Johnson, the club's one-armed professional.

In 1942, Althea began to receive professional coaching at the interracial Cosmopolitan Tennis Club and, a year later, won the New York State Negro Girls Singles title. In 1945 and 1946, she won the National Negro Girls Singles championship and, in 1948, began a decade of domination of the same title in the Women's Division.

Althea completed high school with the help of Dr. Eaton. A year later, she entered Florida A. & M., where she played tennis and basketball for the next four years. In 1950, she was runner-up for the National Indoor Championship and, that same year, became the first African-American to play tennis at Forest Hills, New York. She won the women's singles titles there in 1957 and 1958.

Althea was the first African-American to compete successfully in major international tennis play. She played Wimbledon in England in 1957, winning the women's singles and doubles championships. That same year, she won the women's singles title at the U.S. Open. In 1958, she repeated her Wimbledon and U.S. Open wins. As a tennis professional, she became the world champion in 1960, three years prior to her becoming a professional golfer.

Althea married in 1965 to William A. Darben. She is a member of the Ladies' Professional Golf Association. She is a strong golfer who generally drives 230 to 260 yards off the tee. Mrs. Gibson-Darben has participated in as many as twenty-five tournaments during a single year. However, in recent years she has limited her participation to about six tourneys a season, so that she can devote her time to being recreation supervisor with the Essex County Parks Commission in New Jersey, a job from which she takes considerable satisfaction.

Ambassador

Patricia Roberts Harris

PATRICIA ROBERTS HARRIS
(Born 1924—Died 1985)

Patricia Roberts Harris was the first African-American woman in U.S. history to hold the diplomatic rank of ambassador. She was born in Mattoon, Illinois and attended elementary school in Chicago. She finished her undergraduate studies at Howard University in Washington, D.C., with a summa cum laude B.A. degree in 1945. After completing postgraduate work at the University of Chicago and at American University, she earned her doctorate in jurisprudence from George Washington University Law School in 1960.

Mrs. Harris was admitted to practice before the U.S. Supreme Court and to the District of Columbia bar in 1960. After working for the U.S. Department of Justice for a year, she served as associate dean of students and lecturer in law at Howard University, from 1961 to 1963. In 1963 Harris became professor of law at Howard University, and in 1969 she was made dean of the School of Law. During this period, from 1965 to 1967, she also served as ambassador to Luxembourg.

Following her deanship, Harris joined a Washington, D.C., law firm as a partner. By this time she had received several degrees from institutions throughout the country. A political person as well, she was a delegate to the Democratic National Convention and a presidential elector from the District of Columbia in 1964.

Prior to her appointment as ambassador, Mrs. Harris had worked for the YWCA in Chicago (1946-49), and also served as executive director for Delta Sigma Theta Sorority, Inc. in Washington, D.C. An attorney/professor before she entered politics, Mrs. Harris served under President John F. Kennedy as co-chairman of the National Women's Committee on Civil Rights, and was later named to the Commission on the Status of Puerto Rico.

Mrs. Harris was a Phi Beta Kappa and was also a member of numerous professional and civic organizations. She was made an alternate delegate to the U.N. in 1966.

In 1970, she was named to the board of directors of George-town University, the youngest member in the school's history and only the second African-American to achieve that distinction. Mrs. Harris was elected permanent chairman of the Democratic National Convention on June 27, 1972. In 1977, President Jimmy Carter appointed her to his cabinet as secretary of Housing and Urban Development (HUD).

Because of her extensive experience, Mrs. Harris was in great demand as a member of corporate boards of directors and on governmental task forces. Her lengthy list of achievements includes being named Woman of the Year by the *Ladies' Home Journal,* receiving the Eleanor Roosevelt Humanitarian Award and the Distinguished Service Award of the Council of Jewish Federations, and being inducted into the Order of the Oaken Crown of Luxembourg.

Mrs. Harris died in 1985.

U.S. Representative

Barbara Jordan

BARBARA JORDAN
(Born 1936—Died 1996)

Barbara Jordan was the first African-American woman ever elected to Congress from the Deep South. She was born in Houston, Texas on February 21, 1936. She was the third and youngest daughter of the Reverend Benjamin and Arlynne Jordan. Barbara's parents believed in strict discipline, especially her father, who was a Baptist minister. She and her sisters, Bennie and Rose Mary, were taught respect, dignity, and self-worth. They learned the value of hard work and study. Their father always told them that they could be anything in life, but they had to work hard, so Barbara worked hard. She was almost a straight-A student. Once she received a B and she was not very happy, so she worked to develop "brain power." Her father told her that no one could ever take away a person's brains. Barbara knew that all African-Americans needed to be well educated, because it was the only way to get ahead.

When Barbara was in the tenth grade, she heard a speech by an African-American lawyer from Chicago, Edith Spurlock Sampson. She was very impressed and decided to be a lawyer just like her. Ms. Sampson later became a circuit court judge in Illinois.

Barbara had a burning desire to excel. While in school she played the guitar. In 1952, she graduated at the top of her class from Phillis Wheatley High School. That fall Barbara enrolled at Texas Southern University, an all-African-American school in Houston. There she became a campus leader, scholar, and debate champion. Debating was one of her favorite activities. Barbara was an excellent speaker and had an extensive vocabulary. She enjoyed talking about a subject in public with someone who had a different opinion. She had a strong, clear voice that would fill a room, while everyone watched and listened to her every word. Barbara and her debating team won many awards.

In 1956, she graduated magna cum laude with a B.A. degree in history and political science. Barbara studied law at Boston University in Massachusetts. After graduation from law school in 1959, she could have stayed in Boston and enjoyed an easy life, but she decided to return home. The civil rights movement had started and Barbara wanted to take part in the struggle. As a lawyer, she knew she could help change things.

Starting her law practice was not easy, because she had very little money. So Barbara turned the family dining room into an office. Things were very slow at first, but they soon began to pick up.

Barbara decided that the best way to change things for African-American people was through politics. In 1960, Lyndon Baines Johnson was the vice-presidential candidate from Texas, and he soon became a good friend to Barbara. Barbara proved to be a very good lawyer and people enjoyed her speeches. They liked to hear her talk and she tried to convince everyone that voting was important.

Barbara continued her practice of law in Houston and later became administrative assistant to a county judge. She served in that position until 1962, when she decided to enter politics and run for the Texas State Senate. She continued to work for political and civic causes. More and more people knew who Barbara was and what things she believed in, so this made it easy for her to launch her campaign. However, her decision was very unusual, because no African-American had been elected to the Senate since the days of Reconstruction, after the Civil War (1883).

Barbara ran, but she lost because 1962 was not the right time. She was not happy with the defeat and decided to run again in 1964. She lost again to the same opponent.

Defeat was depressing to Barbara and she considered leaving Texas and going where African-Americans in politics would be accepted. But she decided to stay because she was a Texan and to leave would make her a quitter.

Judge Bill Elliott had been watching Barbara's work, and he knew she was smart so he asked her to be his assistant. This was the first time an African-American was appointed to such a high office in Houston. The job was working with needy people.

Although Barbara liked her work, she still liked politics. She decided to run again for the State Senate in 1966. This time things were different—she won.

In 1967, Barbara Jordan was sworn in as the first African-American state senator since 1883. She was only thirty-one years old. It was a very proud moment. Barbara soon became the most popular senator in the state. She worked on laws that gave farm workers and others the right to earn a minimum wage. Her fellow senators respected and admired her as a freshman senator so much that they paid her a rare tribute for her outstanding work. The city of Houston honored her, too. Mayor Louie Welch proclaimed October 1, 1971 as Barbara Jordan Day.

In 1972, State Sen. Barbara Jordan was elected president pro tempore (temporary president) of the Senate. This meant that she would take over if the governor and lieutenant governor were out of the state. The day they both were, Barbara was sworn in as governor. She was the first African-American woman in United States history to be governor, even for one day.

When Barbara announced she would run for Congress, no one was surprised. She received a great deal of help from friends, including the former president of the United States, Lyndon Baines Johnson. In 1972 she was elected to the U.S. House of Representatives, and she was off to Washington, D.C., the nation's capital.

Barbara had a lot to learn about Congress. She spent many hours reading and studying and attending meetings and conferences. Soon, she was an outstanding legislator, just as she had been in Texas. She also became a member of the Congressional Black Caucus, a group of African-American legislators. In 1974 she was reelected.

Congresswoman Jordan felt strongly about the law and the Constitution. She believed the law should work for all Americans and that no one was above the law.

In 1974, Barbara was part of a committee that was meeting to decide if the president of the United States, Richard Nixon, had covered up the fact that some of his aides had broken the law. President Nixon resigned before the full House of Representatives could act on the recommendations of the committee. In 1974 President Gerald Ford asked Barbara to be one of his personal representatives to Peking, China.

Statement at Debate on Articles of Impeachment, Committee on the Judiciary, House of Representatives, Ninety-third Congress (July 25, 1974):

"We the people," It is a very eloquent beginning. But when that document was completed on the seventeenth of September in 1787 I was not included in that "We, the people." I felt somehow for many years that George Washington and Alexander Hamilton, just left me out by mistake. But through the process of amendment, interpretation and count decision I have finally been included in "We, the people."

By now, Congresswoman Jordan was a popular national figure. She was selected Democratic Woman of the Year by the Women's National Democratic Club. The *Ladies' Home Journal* named Barbara the Woman of the Year in politics. *Time* magazine named her Woman of the Year and in a *Redbook* survey she was named a Woman Who Could be President of the United States.

In 1976, millions of people across the country saw and heard Barbara Jordan give what some considered the most dynamic speech of her career at the National Convention in New York. She received a standing ovation; people were cheering, shouting, and even crying. Many thought she would be a good candidate for vice-president of the United States. But the outstanding legislator liked her job in Congress and decided to stay where she was.

In 1978, after serving three successful terms in the House of Representatives, Barbara retired from public office and returned to Houston. In 1979 she became a public service professor at the University of Texas's Lyndon Baines Johnson School of Public Affairs.

In 1982 she was appointed to a special place of honor called the Lyndon Baines Johnson Centennial Chair in National Policy at the university. She directed a research program on national policy issues. She taught political ethics and intergovernmental relations. As an educator, she had the opportunity to pass along to others her commitment to excellence in government.

Barbara Jordan wrote as well as lectured. She wrote a book about her life experiences. She was also on television as a commentator. Professor Jordan also kept up with her favorite football teams. She was a great fan of the Dallas Cowboys and the Houston Oilers.

In 1984, Barbara Jordan was elected to the Orators Hall of Fame. She served as special advisor on ethics to the governor of Texas.

Civil Rights Activist

Coretta Scott King

CORETTA SCOTT KING
(Born 1927—   )

Coretta Scott King was the first woman to speak at London's St. Paul's Cathedral and at Harvard University's Class Day exercises. She was responsible for establishing the Martin Luther King, Jr. Center for Nonviolent Social Change in Atlanta, and for getting Martin Luther King's birthday declared a national holiday.

Coretta Scott was born on April 27, 1927, in Marion, Alabama. She was the second child born to Obadiah Leonard Scott and Bernice McMurray Scott in the house her father built on his father's farm. Coretta was named after her father's mother, Cora, who was a strong and determined woman. Her entire family was strong, proud, and hardworking and they placed great value on education. Coretta had an older sister named Edythe and a younger brother named Obie. They attended elementary school in a one-room schoolhouse in Heiberger, Alabama, three miles from their home. Coretta's mother wanted her children to get a good education and to try to *be* somebody, so they would not have to depend on anyone for their livelihood.

Coretta attended Lincoln High School, which was founded after the Civil War by the American Missionary Association and located about ten miles from her home. During the 1930s and 1940s there were no schools in the South for African American children. Not many parents were able to send their children to high school, but Coretta's parents were willing to pay $4.50 per year for tuition for each of their three children. Because Lincoln High was so far away from the family farm, Coretta and her siblings had to stay with an African American family who lived closer to the school. Although this living arrangement was expensive,

Coretta's parents had not been able to finish school themselves and they realized how much they had missed. This made them even more determined to provide their children with educational opportunities.

It was while attending Lincoln High School that Coretta's love for music became her primary career interest. Church activities were always very important to her family and Coretta became very involved musically at Mount Tabor AME Zion Church. She led songs, sung solos, and recited poetry. Coretta's music teacher at Lincoln, Olive Williams, gave Coretta her first formal voice lesson. Soon she was singing more than ever, performing individually as well as with the choruses at Lincoln. She took trumpet lessons and learned to play the piano. When Coretta was fifteen, she was asked to be the pianist for the church. She also became the choir director. She developed a format for special church programs, composing narration to go along with the spirituals that were sung. Many years later, Coretta used this same format for the Freedom Concerts she gave.

Coretta graduated as valedictorian from Lincoln High School and received a partial scholarship to the same school her sister was already attending, Antioch College in Yellow Springs, Ohio. Coretta selected elementary education as a major; she was the first African American student to major in this field at Antioch. At this time there were only six African Americans in the whole college. Students majoring in education were required to teach for one year in the Ohio public schools; Coretta decided to teach music. But the school board did not want to have an African American teacher in their public school system, so Coretta was turned down. She had to make a decision to either teach in a segregated African American school in another city or to spend another year at Antioch and teach there. She accepted the latter, but was determined to do something about the situation.

Coretta did not want other people to experience the rejection she had to endure just because of her race. She became involved in organizations and activities that helped people who were mistreated. Antioch had several groups on campus that were involved in promoting race relations and equal rights, including a chapter of the National Association for the Advancement of Colored People (NAACP), a Race Relations Committee, and a Civil Liberties Committee. Coretta joined them all. She also joined a Quaker interest group and took an active role in promoting world peace. She remembered the words she had heard from Horace Mann, the first president of Antioch: "Be ashamed to all until you have won some victory for humanity." She was determined to do something for all people.

Coretta became very serious about her study of music at Antioch. Walter F. Anderson, the only African American faculty member there, coached her before her first public concert, which was given at the Second Baptist Church in Springfield, Ohio, in 1948. Coretta was very fortunate to appear in a program with Paul Robeson, who encouraged her to continue developing her talent. It was at that point that Coretta decided to attend a music conservatory after completing college to specialize in voice, in order to develop hers to its fullest potential. Coretta received a B.A. degree in music and elementary education from Antioch and was accepted at the New England Conservatory of Music in Boston, Massachusetts.

After graduation, Corretta went to the conservatory and became friendly with a student named Mary Powell. Mary was a matchmaker; she gave Corretta's telephone number to a young man named Martin Luther King, Jr. The next day Martin called Coretta and they met for lunch. Martin was a student at Boston University, working on his doctorate in theology.

On June 18, 1953, Martin's father, affectionately known as Daddy King, married Coretta and Martin. The wedding took place on the lawn of Coretta's parents' new home in Alabama, next to their general store. The following Sunday, Martin preached at his father's church, Ebenezer Baptist, in Atlanta, Georgia. Martin introduced Coretta to the congregation; she joined the church and was baptized. Coretta began working as a clerk at the Atlanta Citizens Trust Company, where Daddy King was a director. Coretta and Martin lived in Martin's parents' house all summer because they had plans to go back to school to continue their studies. They returned to Boston and found an apartment near where Martin used to live.

In March of 1954, Martin was asked to become the pastor of Dexter Avenue Baptist Church in Montgomery, Alabama. After much consideration and discussion Coretta and Martin decided to return to the South to be a part of the changes that were taking place for African American people. Coretta realized Martin had an intense conviction and concern for humanity, which brought her a measure of self-realization early in their relationship. She sensed Martin's incredible dynamism so she had no regrets at the prospect of relinquishing her own career dreams. Coretta told Martin if this was what he wanted, then she would try to make herself happy.

They subsequently moved to Montgomery. They met another young African American minister, Ralph Abernathy, and his wife, Juanita. Ralph and Juanita were also committed to social reform, so Martin invited Ralph to preach at Dexter Avenue Baptist Church. Coretta acted as Martin's secretary and worked on various church committees. In the spring of 1955, Martin received his Ph.D. in theology from Boston University and Coretta discovered that she was pregnant.

On November 17, 1955, their daughter, Yolanda, who they called Yoki for short, was born. Their lives seemed complete, but a few weeks later an African American woman named Rosa Parks helped change their lives forever. Mrs. Parks had refused to give up her seat in a whites-only section of the city bus she was riding, and was consequently arrested. Mr. Edgar Daniel Nixon, president of the Montgomery branch of the NAACP, contacted all the African American ministers and community leaders in the city to plan a strategy for staging a Montgomery bus boycott. This incident gave birth to a new era of Civil Rights agitation, and Coretta and Dr. King were directly involved. Two years later Dr. King became head of the Southern Christian Leadership Conference (SCLC).

On October 23, 1957, Coretta and Martin's second child, Martin Luther King, III, was born. On January 30, 1961, Coretta

74

gave birth to Dexter Scott King; and on March 28, 1963, Bernice Albertine King was born. Coretta's primary focus was on raising her children. Although in 1962 Coretta served as a voice instructor in the music department of Morris Brown College in Atlanta, during the period of Martin's public career, Coretta usually remained out of the public spotlight. Over the years Coretta gradually became more involved in Martin's work, singing spirituals at events where he spoke and filling in as speaker when he was not able to appear. She also became involved in activities that did not include her husband, such as in 1962 when she served as a delegate for Women's Strike for Peace to the seventeen-nation Disarmament in Geneva, Switzerland. In the mid 1960s she sung, recited poetry, and lectured, demonstrating the history of the Civil Rights movement at the Multi-Arts Freedom Concerts that raised money for SCLC.

After the assassination of her husband on April 4, 1968, in Memphis, Tennessee, Coretta devoted her life to actively propagating her husband's philosophy of nonviolence. At first she started to fill many of the commitments his death left undone, but soon she became sought after in her own right. Coretta's speech on Solidarity Day, June 19, 1968, was often identified as a prime example of her emergence from the shadow of her husband's memory. In her speech Coretta called upon American women to unite and form a solid block of woman power to fight the three great evils: racism, poverty, and war. Much of her subsequent activity revolved around building plans for the creation of a Martin Luther King, Jr. Memorial in Atlanta, which she began working on in 1969. (The memorial was established under the auspices of the National Park Service in 1980.) Also in 1969, she began mobilizing support for the Martin Luther King, Jr. Center for Nonviolent Social Change.

Coretta's activism extended beyond the United States. For example, in the mid-1980s, she and two of her children were arrested for demonstrating against apartheid outside of the South African Embassy in Washington, D.C. The following year, 1986, she visited South Africa and met with businessmen and anti-apartheid leaders. Coretta has also decried the human rights violations of the Haitian military regime against Haitian citizens. In 1983, she implored the United Nations to re-impose an embargo against the nation.

Coretta has had to deal with a lot of controversy. The Center for Non-Violent Social Change became involved in a terrible struggle with the National Park Service over the issue of how best to utilize some of the historic district in Atlanta where the King memorials are located. As CEO of the center, Coretta was forced to mediate between her family's desire for an interactive museum with exhibitions and programs for youngsters and the National Park Service's plan for a visitor's center on the same site. The dispute was not resolved until April of 1995, a few months after Coretta officially stepped down, handing the reigns over to her son, Dexter, who was unanimously voted in as the director and CEO of the center.

Controversy continued. In 1964, Dr. King gave nearly eighty-three thousand documents, including correspondence and other manuscripts, to Boston University. Coretta had hoped to regain control of that legacy, but in April 1995, the Massachusetts Supreme Judicial Court ruled in favor of the university, leaving Coretta and many other Atlantans displeased.

Coretta remains an eloquent and respected spokesperson on behalf of black causes and nonviolent philosophy. She is recognized for keeping her husband's dream alive. In September 1995, Coretta and two other famous civil rights widows, Mylie Evers-Williams and Betty Shabazz, were honored by the National Political Congress of Black Women.

Coretta still resides in Atlanta and is involved in various causes such as those supported by the National Organization for Women, the Women's International League for Peace and Freedom, and United Church Women. She remains committed to training a new generation about Dr. King's philosophy of bringing about social change through nonviolence.

Educator

Elizabeth Duncan Koontz

ELIZABETH DUNCAN KOONTZ
(Born 1919—Died 1989)

Elizabeth Koontz was the first African-American woman to be elected president of the Association of Classroom Teachers and later became the first African-American president of the NEA (National Education Association). She was born in Salisbury, North Carolina. In 1938 she graduated with honors from Livingstone College, and in 1941 she earned a master's degree in education from Atlanta University. She then studied at Columbia University, Indiana University, and North Carolina College. Mrs. Koontz has received many honorary degrees.

Elizabeth was born the youngest of seven children and was reared by well-educated parents who instilled in their offspring an appreciation for the values of formal education. Like the rest of the family, Elizabeth was attracted to a teaching career, taking her first job in the small lumber town of Dunn, North Carolina, where she found herself tackling a big assignment with no experience. She quickly developed what would become a lifelong interest in supposedly "mentally retarded" children, whom she herself generally classifies as slow learners needing only patience and understanding so they will develop at the same rate of perception and level of skill as other less-neglected pupils.

Mrs. Koontz became head of North Carolina's all-African-American NEA affiliate, as well as the association's largest division, the 820,000-member-strong Association of Classroom Teachers. In 1968, she became president of the 1.1

million-member NEA. Once in office as NEA head, she made it clear that she anticipated trouble as soon as teachers began to organize, agitate, and strike for higher pay and improved conditions. When the NEA did in fact stage strikes, she advised communities to adjust to teachers' demands, and to support bona fide attempts to upgrade the calibre of teaching candidates by making the profession more lucrative.

In 1969 President Richard M. Nixon appointed Mrs. Koontz director of the Women's Bureau of the U.S. Department of Labor, the first major appointment of an African-American in the Nixon Administration. Mrs. Koontz remained in this post until 1972. Her involvement in women's liberation was consistent with her reputation as a fighting lady equally adept at practicing both careful, soothing tact and decisive, outspoken bluntness.

Sculptor

Edmonia Lewis

EDMONIA LEWIS
(Born 1845—Died 1890)

Edmonia Lewis was the first African-American woman to gain wide recognition as a sculptor. Her contribution in the fine arts is considered very important both aesthetically and historically.

Ms. Lewis was born in 1845 in Albany, New York. Her mother was a full-blooded Chippewa Indian and her father was a free full-blooded African-American. Her parents died when she was very young. After living for three years with the Chippewa, Edmonia's older brother sought to have her educated. From 1859 to 1863, under the patronage of a number of abolitionists, she was educated at Oberlin Preparatory College in Ohio. Oberlin College was the first American institution of higher learning to admit women on a nonsegregated basis. While at Oberlin Ms. Lewis became interested in sculpture.

After completing her schooling she moved to Boston, where she developed her interest in sculpture. With the help of abolitionist William Lloyd Garrison she studied under Edmund Brackett, a noted sculptor. While there she met Col. Robert Gould Shaw, the commander of the first African-American regiment raised in the state of Massachusetts during the Civil War, and she did a bust of him. Ms. Lewis's exhibit of the bust of Col. Robert G. Shaw in 1865 made it possible for her to study in Rome.

In Rome, Ms. Lewis specialized in portrait busts. She soon became a prominent figure in the American art colony there. She set up a studio and went on to fame as a sculptor.

Resembling an East Indian in appearance, Ms. Lewis possessed "an appealing intensity and forthrightness." In Rome she was an exotic sight, wearing mannish garb and hacking directly from marble the images she had created in her mind. Most of her adult career was spent in Italy.

Returning to the United States she fulfilled many commissions, including a bust of Henry Wadsworth Longfellow, which was placed in Wilderner Library at Harvard University in 1869. Riding the crest of the neoclassical revival in the 1870s, she attracted wide notice in artistic circles. Ms. Lewis did portrait busts of a number of the prominent figures of her era. Among her best-known works are a medallion head of John Brown, a fine plaster portrait of Charles Sumner, and busts of Abraham Lincoln and Wendell Phillips.

Ms. Lewis also executed a large number of complete figures and groups. *Hagar in the Wilderness* (1866), depicting a biblical theme; *Hiawatha* (1865), *The Marriage of Hiawatha* (1865), and *The Departure of Hiawatha*, on the famous Indian legend; *Madonna and Child* (1867); and *The Death of Cleopatra* (1867) are among her better works. Though less technically accomplished than her bust of Charles Sumner, for example, a remarkably modern-looking mother-and-children group called *Forever Free* (1867) aroused the greatest general interest. This particular group shows an African-American couple, just out of slavery, becoming aware of the fact that they are no longer in bondage. *Forever Free* was made for the Harriet Hunt Mausoleum in Cambridge, Massachusetts.

As her skill and fame grew, Ms. Lewis exhibited her work in Chicago in 1870, in Rome in 1871, and at the Centennial Celebration in Philadelphia in 1876, where she and Richard Bannister, also an African-American, received top honors.

During the 1880s, the vogue of neoclassicism was passing. Ms. Lewis also passed from public notice, and her last years were very obscured. She died in Rome in 1890.

Her work was exhibited at the Art of the American Negro Exhibition, Chicago, in 1940; at Howard University, Washington,

D.C., in 1967; at Vassar College, Poughkeepsie, New York in 1972; and elsewhere. Ms. Lewis is represented in the collections of the Frederick Douglass Institute of African American Arts and History, Washington, D.C. and of the Harvard College Library, Cambridge, Massachusetts.

Actress

Hattie McDaniel

HATTIE McDANIEL
(Born 1898—Died 1952)

Hattie McDaniel was the first African-American woman to win an Oscar from the Academy of Motion Pictures, Arts, and Sciences. She won in the best supporting actress category for her performance in *Gone with the Wind.*

Ms. McDaniel was born on June 10, 1898 in Wichita, Kansas and moved to Denver, Colorado as a child. After singing on Denver radio as an amateur for some time, she entered vaudeville professionally and, by 1924, was a headliner on the Pantages circuit.

By 1931, she had made her way to Hollywood, where, after a slow start, she gradually began to get some movie roles. Meanwhile she supported herself as a maid and washer woman. *Judge Priest, The Little Colonel,* and *Showboat* were some of the movies in which she appeared, along with *Saratoga* and *Nothing Sacred.* Her portrayal of a "mammy" figure in *Gone with the Wind* is regarded as a kind of definitive interpretation of this role.

Gone with the Wind, David O. Selznick's expensive film of Margaret Mitchell's best-selling novel, was the best film depiction of its time of the African-American plight on the eve of the Civil War. Butterfly Queen appeared as an urbane Easterner, and *Time* reported that in her shrill role she went beyond mere servitude toward "sly humor." While pretending to be the perfect servant, she would put her employers in their place without acting subservient. The African-American press plugged Hattie McDaniel's Mammy for its "dignity and earnestness" that would raise her to "more than a servant." The film's gaudy premiere, its reception, and the eventual Academy Award given to Ms. McDaniel polarized African-American opinion for and against the picture. Some people admired the work of the African-Americans in the movie, while others felt that the roles were degrading. Even the Communist party was divided on the subject. Thenceforth, African-American roles in film slowly improved.

In 1942, the trade paper *Variety* printed a headline reading, *Better Breaks for Negroes in H'wood*. The story referred to an agreement struck by major studio heads, Walter White of the NAACP, and Wendell Willkie, the defeated Republican presidential candidate in 1940, through which African-Americans could expect better roles—roles that would portray how African-Americans might normally appear in society, and that would depart from the old stereotypes. Ad hoc committees of African-American actors and citizens, liberal white groups, and the African-American press became micrometers for measuring the studios' cleaving to the new standards. Organized African-Americans gave awards to movies that took liberal stances.

By then African-Americans were at the mercy of Hollywood because race movies were slow to disappear. The one exception to white productions was the "soundies," short musical films starring many African-Americans produced for use in jukeboxes. Fritz Pollard, an old African-American football star, fronted the organization but gradually it fell under white control.

In addition to her movie roles, Ms. McDaniel had ample success on radio during the 1930s, particularly as "Hi-Hat Hattie." In the 1940s she played the title character of the very successful "Beulah" series.

Ms. McDaniel died on October 26, 1952.

Federal Judge

Constance Baker Motley

CONSTANCE BAKER MOTLEY
(Born about 1921—   )

Constance Motley was the first female African-American federal judge and the first African-American woman to be elected to the New York Senate. Two years after winning her Senate seat, she was appointed by President Lyndon B. Johnson to the U.S. District Court for Southern New York, in 1966. The appointment marked the high point of her long career in politics and civic affairs.

Constance was born in New Haven, Connecticut to West Indian parents. She attended Fisk University in Nashville, Tennessee for a time, and received a B.A. degree from New York University in 1943 and her law degree from Columbia University in 1946. Even before her graduation from law school, she joined the National Association for the Advancement of Colored People Legal Defense and Educational Fund, Inc., and remained with it until 1964.

Before leaving the organization to run for the New York State Senate, Mrs. Motley had argued nine successful NAACP cases before the U.S. Supreme Court, having participated in almost every important civil rights case that had passed through the courts since 1954. She represented James Meredith in his efforts to gain admission to the University of Mississippi.

By winning the election to the State Senate in February of 1964, Mrs. Motley became the only woman among fifty-eight senators and the first African-American woman in New York state history to sit in the upper chamber.

One year later, Mrs. Motley ran for the position of Manhattan borough president, emerging the victor by the unanimous final vote of the City Council. She thus became the first woman to serve as a city borough president, and also the first woman on the Board of Estimates.

In June 1982, Judge Motley was named chief judge of the federal district court that covers Manhattan, the Bronx, and six counties north of New York City. She succeeded Judge Lloyd F. MacMahony, who relinquished his administrative duties.

Judge Motley is a resident of Manhattan's Upper West Side, where she lives with her husband and son. She uses the courts and law as her weapons and hopes that her career "will be an inspiration to other African-American women." She feels that "it is important for women, and especially African-American women, to become involved and to hold public office."

Civil Rights Activist

Rosa Parks

ROSA PARKS
(Born 1913—   )

Rosa Parks was the first African-American woman to spark the civil rights movement. She is considered the heroine of the bus boycott. Her refusal to give a white man her seat on a bus in Montgomery, Alabama became one of the most significant acts in African-American history.

Rosa McCauley was born in Tuskegee, Alabama, in 1913 and grew up on a small farm with her brother, mother, and grandparents. She attended an all-African-American school that closed three months earlier than white schools so that the children could work in the fields.

When Rosa turned eleven, her mother had saved enough money to send her to a private school in Montgomery. She attended high school until her mother became ill. After quitting school, Rosa found a job as a house servant and began sending money back to her family in Tuskegee. When she married Raymond Parks, she returned to high school and graduated.

In 1943 she joined the NAACP and worked to ensure voting rights for African-Americans. She continued to work for the NAACP while she held various jobs as housecleaner, seamstress, and office clerk.

On the evening of December 1, 1955, Mrs. Parks boarded a public bus in Montgomery. She took a seat with the other passengers, and prepared to relax before arriving home. Soon there were no seats left. When the white bus driver noticed that an African-American woman was occupying a seat in the "white" section of the bus while a white passenger was standing, he ordered the "offender" to the rear. Mrs. Parks simply did not move.

Mrs. Parks was arrested, jailed, and brought to trial while the rest of the once quiet African-American community refused to ride public buses for 381 days. Mrs. Parks was the catalyst in the Montgomery boycott. This was the first time most people had heard of Dr. Martin Luther King, Jr. His church, Dexter Avenue Baptist Church in Montgomery, was where the boycott was organized.

Mrs. Parks paid dearly for her courage. Her husband, a barber, became ill from the pressure; the family ultimately moved to Detroit, where Mr. Parks resumed his profession. Mrs. Parks did sewing and alterations at home until she found a job as a dressmaker.

In Detroit, she has since become active in youth work, job guidance, cultural and recreational planning—the daily grind of a community activist. Dr. King, while he lived, once called her "the great fuse that led to the modern stride toward freedom." She made the stride while sitting still.

Mrs. Parks is presently a receptionist-secretary to Cong. John Conyers. A religious person, she serves as deaconess of St. Matthews A.M.E. Church in Detroit. She accepts many speaking engagements because she wants to help "young people grow, develop, and reach their potential."

Opera Singer

Leontyne Price

LEONTYNE PRICE
(Born 1927—   )

Leontyne Price became the first African-American to appear in an opera on television. She sang the title role in an NBC production of *Tosca*.

Leontyne was born Mary Leontyne Price in Laurel, Mississippi. She began taking piano lessons when she was five years old. She did not mind leaving her friends and coming inside to practice, because she loved playing the piano. At an early age it was clear that Leontyne had musical talent. Her mother, who was a gifted singer in the church choir, wanted to do everything she could to develop her daughter's talent. She involved Leontyne in music at home, school, and church. Music soon became Leontyne's life. On her sixth birthday her parents had saved enough money to buy her a secondhand piano. That year she was presented in her first piano recital.

At Sandy Gavin Elementary School, Leontyne learned dancing and acrobatics from her third-grade teacher. She loved performing and was often the star in many of the school programs. She was an A student.

When Leontyne was nine years old, her mother took her by bus to Jackson, Mississippi to hear Marian Anderson in concert. Marian Anderson was the first African-American singer to appear at New York City's Metropolitan Opera and Leontyne was thrilled and inspired. She decided that she wanted to be a performer like Marian Anderson when she grew up.

Leontyne attended Oak Park Vocational High School, where she sang first soprano with the Oak Park Choral Group. She also played piano in many school, church, and community concerts. Before Leontyne graduated from school she appeared in a solo recital, singing as well as playing the piano. She graduated with honors and was presented with an award for outstanding ability in music.

Leontyne's parents were convinced that she should continue her education, so they arranged for her to attend Wilberforce College in Ohio. Even though she had a scholarship, she worked part time to help with the expenses. When Leontyne began college she had no idea of the full potential of her vocal ability. Her goal at that time was to get a degree and teach music, so that she could help out at home and help pay her brother's way through college.

Ms. Price was encouraged by her voice coach, Catherine Van Buren, to obtain the advanced vocal training that was needed to develop her voice properly. After graduating from college, she competed for and won a scholarship to the renowned Juilliard School of Music in New York City. Shortly after Ms. Price entered Juilliard she became seriously interested in opera. For four years she studied under the direction of Florence Page Kimball, her first formal voice teacher. Ms. Price appeared in many of the school's concerts and operatic productions. During one of these performances at Juilliard, Virgil Thomson heard her sing and asked her to sing the role of St. Cecelia in his opera *Four Saints in Three Acts*. This brief Broadway appearance was so successful that Ms. Price was signed to sing the role of Bess in George Gershwin's folk opera *Porgy and Bess*. This made her more determined to succeed in grand opera.

Ms. Price made successful debuts in grand opera productions in Europe. She conquered audiences in Paris, Vienna, and London as well as in the United States. Following these triumphs, she was invited to star at the Metropolitan Opera in New York. When she finished singing the role of Leonora in Verdi's *Il Trovatore,* the audience gave her the longest tribute of applause in the Metropolitan Opera's history. The ovation lasted forty-two minutes. Later she became the first African-American artist to have the honor of opening a Metropolitan

Opera season. She starred in the opera written by Samuel Barber, *Anthony and Cleopatra,* that opened at the new opera house, the $50 million Metropolitan Opera House at Lincoln Center.

Ms. Price gave her farewell operatic performance on January 3, 1985, at the Metropolitan Opera. She sang the title role in Verdi's *Aida* in a performance that was telecast live from Lincoln Center. This ended her operatic appearances but it did not end her singing career. With her brother, George, as her manager, Leontyne continues to give concert performances.

Ms. Price has received many awards and honors. In 1964 she received the highest American civilian award, the Presidential Freedom Medal, from President Lyndon B. Johnson. She has received the NAACP Spingarn Medal for high and noble achievement by an African-American. She has been featured on magazine covers, and her recordings have received eighteen Grammy awards from the National Academy of Recording Arts and Sciences. She has received three Emmy Awards for her work in television. She also helps to provide music lessons to children in Harlem (New York) at prices they can afford. Ms. Price's children's book, *Aïda,* won the Coretta Scott King Award for Excellence in 1990.

Olympic Gold Medalist

Wilma Rudolph

WILMA RUDOLPH
(Born 1940—   )

Wilma Rudolph was the first African-American woman to win three gold medals in track in a single Olympics. Her performance is all the more remarkable because she was unable to walk properly until she was eight years old.

Wilma was born on June 20, 1940 in St. Bethlehem, Tennessee. She soon moved with the family to Clarksville, where she would spend her childhood.

During this time the United States was just emerging from the Great Depression, but Wilma's parents were more fortunate than some. Her father was a railroad porter and handyman, and her mother took in laundry and sewing and worked occasionally as a maid. Wilma was the twentieth child born to Blanche and Ed Rudolph. Their little house had no bathroom—only an outhouse a few steps from their back door. New store-bought clothes were rare. Wilma and her brothers and sisters usually wore clothes their mother made for them from patterned flour sacks.

Wilma's first great accomplishment was living to see her first birthday. She was born nearly two months early, because of a fall her mother suffered during pregnancy. At birth Wilma weighed only four and a half pounds and for a while, it did not look as if she would survive. In 1940 only about half of the babies born weighing fewer than five pounds survived and the best medical care was available to very few in those days.

There was poor medical care for African-Americans and in Wilma's early years she needed quite a bit of medical attention. She battled against the common childhood diseases that were deadly then, before there were vaccines and drugs to fight them. In her first three years of life, she suffered from measles, mumps, and chicken pox. At age four, she nearly died during a long struggle, first with double pneumonia, then with scarlet fever.

Wilma finally recovered but there was something wrong with her left leg. It was crooked and her foot was turned inward. When her mother took her to the doctor, she was told that her daughter must have contracted polio during her last long sickness. The doctor told her mother that Wilma would never walk, but her mother told her she would.

Beginning in 1946, Wilma and her mother traveled twice a week to Meharry Medical College, fifty miles away in Nashville, where she would undergo physical therapy, which included exercise and massage sessions to strengthen her paralyzed leg. Her family members took turns massaging her leg daily.

Wilma's infirmity prevented her from sharing in the fun that most children took for granted. Her family cheered her on as she struggled to regain use of her wasted limb, and saw her through the pain of her numerous setbacks during her recovery. Wilma repaid her family for their help through her courage, her refusal to acknowledge pain, and her playful disposition.

Wilma's weak leg made it difficult for her to attend school, so a tutor periodically came out to her home. The rest of the time her mother and older sisters and brothers filled in, helping her to master the basics of math and reading. Finally, when Wilma was seven years old, she could walk steadily enough on her leg brace to enter the Cook Elementary School. The next year, a special left shoe helped her to get around. At the end of Wilma's sixth-grade year in school, she did not have to wear her brace anymore.

In 1952, twelve-year-old Wilma finally achieved her dream of shedding her handicap and becoming more like other children. She decided she would make her mark on the basketball court. Her mother tried to discourage her from pursuing sports, but Wilma could not be stopped.

When she entered Burt High School in Clarksville, basketball became the center of Wilma's life. She discovered that she could move with grace and style. She was fast, sure of her footing, and growing taller every day.

Wilma's older sister, Yvonne, played on the school's girls' basketball team, and Wilma vowed to follow in her footsteps. Wilma became a new star. Playing on the team gave her an opportunity to attend college and to travel the globe as a world-class athlete, all expenses paid.

In 1956, Ed Temple invited Wilma to spend the summer living and training with other promising high-school athletes at Tennessee State University. Mr. Temple believed that with her speed, Wilma could excel in track events. She spent the summer working hard on critical elements of running that she had never thought about before—breathing, starts, and race strategy.

Wilma ran in the Amateur Athletic Union (AAU) competition held in Philadelphia and she was victorious. A few weeks later she was driven across the country to qualify for the Olympic track team, and became its youngest member. In Melbourne, Australia, in 1956, the U.S. women's 400-meter relay team won the Olympic bronze medal, the third-place prize. Wilma regretted her loss in the women's 100-meter dash, but she was thrilled by the team's success.

At the age of seventeen, Wilma was expecting a child by her boyfriend, Robert Eldridge. He later became her husband. Her sister, Yvonne, agreed to take her child into her household until Wilma could care for a family full time. Her coach, Mr. Temple, told her he would waive his standing rule against allowing mothers in his training program at Tennessee State. So Wilma finished out her senior year in high school, graduating in June 1958. A month later she gave birth to a baby girl, whom she named Yolanda.

That September Wilma entered Tennessee State on a full athletic scholarship. She found the adjustment to college very difficult, but she was determined not to allow motherhood to interfere with her education and training. She accepted Coach

Temple's discipline and learned to juggle her different roles. Wilma made the track team her freshman year. At the beginning of her crucial sophomore year, the year of the trials for the 1960 Olympic Games, she began to lose races regularly to her three other Tigerbelle teammates. The team doctor discovered that Wilma had a persistent tonsil infection that had been taking her strength. After she had her tonsils removed, Wilma soon regained her position as the fastest of the Tigerbelles.

In August 1960, Wilma won the 100- and 200-meter dashes at the Olympic trials, securing a place on the U.S. team. Ed Temple was named coach of the U.S. Olympic women's track team. The 1960 Olympic Games were to be held in Rome, and Wilma's goal of winning three gold medals was almost within grasp. The Tuesday before the competition, she suffered an injury. She was jogging across a field when she hit a small hollow spot and fell, popping her ankle. According to the doctor, her ankle seemed to be strained, not sprained or broken. He told her to keep off it for a few days. Fortunately her injury responded to the rest, and she was well enough to compete in the 100- and 200-meter dashes.

Wilma won both races and her team won the 400-meter relay. Wilma received three Olympic gold medals. She was considered the fastest woman in the world. When she returned home, a police motorcade escorted her to Clarksville for the victory party. The homecoming banquet was the first racially integrated event in the town's history. Wilma's spectacular achievements had brought the people of Clarksville together.

By the beginning of 1961, Wilma had received many of the world's most prestigious athletic awards. The Associated Press named her Woman Athlete of the Year. She became the first American to win Italy's Christopher Columbus Award as the most outstanding international sports personality. A group of European sportswriters even named her "Sportsman of the Year," making her the first woman ever to win that title. Amid all the success, Wilma returned to Tennessee State to finish her degree in elementary education. She also took a part-time job working at the university post office, and she hoped to spend more time with her family. But honors and invitations continued to stream in, many too exciting to ignore.

Wilma's fame enabled her to open doors that had long been closed to female athletes. Track competition was a male-dominated world where women, whatever they achieved, were still considered second class. Wilma's stardom broke down the barriers of gender. She was the first woman to compete in the prestigious New York Athletic Club meet, the Penn Relays, and the Los Angeles Times Games.

In July 1961, Wilma was invited to Moscow, the capital of the Soviet Union. There she equaled her previous world record for the 100-meter dash and anchored the victorious American women's relay team. And the awards kept coming, including the 1961 James E. Sullivan Award, given to "the amateur athlete" who by performance, example, and good influence did the most to advance good sportsmanship throughout the year. Wilma was stunned by the invitation to the White House and asked her mother and Coach Temple to accompany her.

In 1962, Wilma had a major race slated in a meet pitting U.S. athletes against runners from the Soviet Union. She trained extensively for the competition to be held at California's Stanford University. She won the 100-meter dash and won the relay race.

After this competition Wilma knew it was time to retire. She took off her track shoes, signed her name on both of them, and gave them to a little boy who asked her for her autograph. She left while she was still on top, the same year she won the Babe Didrikson Zaharias Award, given to the most outstanding female athlete in the world.

Although Wilma retired from competition, she continued to serve as a goodwill ambassador. In May 1963, she represented the U.S. State Department at the Games of Friendship, the largest track-and-field event ever held in Africa.

Wilma returned home to Tennessee to find two job offers waiting for her. She was asked to take over the position of Coach Gray, who was killed in an automobile accident, as the

Burt High School track coach that fall and also to teach second grade at the former elementary school. Wilma now had the chance to build a personal life—something the rigors of athletics had long prevented. Through all her years of training, of single-minded dedication, her boyfriend, Robert Eldridge, had been waiting. Finally, in the summer of 1963 they were married. By the time of the 1960 Olympic Games, Wilma had given birth to her second daughter, Djuana. The following year she had her first son, Robert Jr.

Wilma later accepted a job in Evansville, Indiana, as director of a community center. From there she and her family moved to Poland Spring, Maine, where she would manage the girls' physical education section of a government-sponsored recreation program. Then in 1967, Vice-President Hubert Humphrey invited Wilma to participate in "Operation Camp," a project that trained young athletes in America's sixteen largest ghettos. She traveled with other athletes to cities across the nation, teaching track and inspiring hope in young people whose chances had been limited by poverty and prejudice.

Later Wilma became pregnant with her fourth child. Xurry, her second son, was born in 1971. In the early 1970s, Wilma organized athletic programs for Mayor Daley's Youth Foundation in Chicago. Later she served as an administrator for several learning institutions and did public relations work for banks. She modeled occasionally.

Wilma got tired of having her celebrity exploited and being expected to function primarily as a figurehead, so she started her own company, Wilma Unlimited, in the late 1970s. The founding of the company made her take a firm hold of her own future. She became a one-woman corporation. She began traveling around the country, inspiring others with the story of her setbacks and successes.

In 1977 she acted as a consultant during the filming of a television movie based on her autobiography, *Wilma*, which was published the same year. In 1981, she started the Wilma Rudolph Foundation, a nonprofit organization dedicated to training young athletes. The organization is based in

112

Indianapolis, and had over a thousand participants by the mid-1980s. The organization provides its members with free coaching in their chosen sports, and it prepares talented athletes for AAU meets, national sports festivals, and even the Olympics. She later accepted a position as special consultant on minority affairs at De Pauw University in Indiana.

Abolitionist

Sojourner Truth

SOJOURNER TRUTH
(Born about 1797—Died 1883)

Sojourner Truth was the first African-American woman to speak out publicly against slavery. Isabella Baumfree—or Sojourner Truth, as she is popularly known—became famous in her lifetime as a preacher, abolitionist, and lecturer.

There is no exact record of Sojourner's birthday, but it was probably about 1797. She was born about fourteen years after the end of the American Revolution. Her original name was Isabella and her mother and father called her Belle. "Sojourner Truth" was a name she made up for herself, because it meant sojourner or traveler on earth and one who spoke the truth. That was the creed she had made for herself—the way of life she followed.

The first home she ever knew was the grim, dark cellar of a stately limestone house on the plantation of Charles Hardenbergh in Hurley, a town about eighty miles north of New York City. Her parents had ten children; Belle was the ninth child. The first language that she learned was Dutch.

In 1806 Belle was sold to John Neely. She was beaten because she spoke Dutch and the Neelys spoke English so they did not understand a single word she spoke. She carried scars of the beatings for the rest of her life.

In 1814 Belle married a slave named Thomas. The marriage was arranged by her slave master. They lived together for about ten years. During that time she had five children, four of whom lived through infancy. Their names were Diana, Peter, Elizabeth, and Sophia.

In 1817, three years after her marriage, Belle heard that the

New York state legislature had passed a law that decreed all New York slaves born before July 4, 1799 would be freed on July 4, 1827. In 1799, a law had been passed that stated all slaves born before 1799 on would be free after they became twenty-five years old. Because Belle was not yet twenty-five, and it was not 1827 yet, she was not to be freed that year.

With just one of her children, Belle escaped from Mr. Dumont, her master at the time. She felt that no matter what happened to her she would never be a slave again. She carried Sophia in one arm and held a pillowcase of her belongings in the other, with no money, home, food, or destination.

Belle kept walking and realized she was near the home of Levi Rowe, a man who had offered to help her years ago. His intentions were the same, but now he was sick and bedridden. He told her to go to the home of Isaac and Maria Van Wagener. They were a Quaker couple who lived a few miles away.

Belle arrived at their home and told Mrs. Van Wagener that Levi Rowe sent her. Mrs. Van Wagener gave Belle and her baby something to eat. After Belle told the couple about her life and how the laws still would not allow her to be freed, they offered her a job and a place to sleep. A few hours later, Mr. Dumont found Belle and demanded that she come back with him. Mr. Van Wagener made Mr. Dumont an offer and was able to buy Belle's freedom for twenty dollars and Sophia's for five dollars.

Belle was the first African-American woman to sue a white man, and she won the freedom of her son, Peter. She had faced down slave dealers in a white man's court and won justice for her son. Ms. Gear, a schoolteacher, came to Kingston, where Belle lived now, and became interested in Peter's education. Ms. Gear talked Belle into coming to New York City with her son, so Peter could go to school. Belle had to make a decision, so she decided to leave her baby Sophia with friends so Peter could go to school. Ms. Gear raised the money to pay for Peter's expenses and she helped Belle find housework, so Belle could pay for her room and board.

Belle became one of the followers of a religious leader by the name of Elijah Pierson. His church was called the "Kingdom of

God." Soon Belle realized what a terrible mistake she made by joining the "Kingdom" and giving up her freedom of choice. One day when she was in Pierson's house, he suddenly became delirious, then paralyzed. Within hours Pierson was dead and Belle was implicated, although never accused, in an alleged murder plot. Her name was finally cleared, but something good came from this bad experience. For the first time in her life she spoke in front of a white audience. It was a turning point for her because it was the first time she realized the power of speech that was at her command. She preached about slavery and how it took many forms. She opened people's eyes to the oppression that could be seen everywhere.

Belle spoke to God constantly. She heard powerful voices telling her that she had a mission to help the needy and the oppressed. Early in the summer of 1843, she decided to act on God's command that she leave New York City and become a traveling preacher. At age forty-six, she headed east toward Long Island.

She felt free, as though she was repeating the escape from slavery that she had made years before. Belle felt it was impossible to carry her old name on the new journey. She wanted a new name, a free woman's name, a name that had never been attached to a slave master of any kind. Calling on God for help in choosing her new name, she received an answer; she called herself "Sojourner." One day on her journey a lady asked her what her last name was. Once again she prayed for guidance, and the answer that came to her was "Truth." She thought it was a very suitable name for one of God's pilgrims. A "sojourner" was a traveler who only rested temporarily, never staying in one place too long. The last name was her creed: "truth." With only two shillings tucked into the pocket of her long dress, she left Long Island and proceeded northward, preaching in Connecticut and Massachusetts. Wherever she went, people flocked to listen to her.

In the winter of 1843, Sojourner needed a place to live. Some friends she had met on the road introduced her to a group called the Northampton Association of Education and

Industry, in Florence, Massachusetts. The Northampton Association was a utopian community founded by a number of professors, abolitionists, idealists, and workers. The purpose of the community, as stated in its charter, was to "pursue truth, justice, humanity, the equality of rights and rank for all." The abolitionist movement sought to put an end to slavery. William Lloyd Garrison frequently visited the association.

In 1831 Garrison had founded an influential antislavery newspaper, the *Liberator,* and he had formed the New England Anti-Slavery Society during the following year. By 1846, the Northampton Association had disbanded, and Sojourner Truth took up housekeeping work for George Benson and other abolitionist organizers in the area.

Between 1846 and 1850 Sojourner Truth became increasingly involved in the antislavery crusade. During these years something changed deeply in Sojourner Truth. She no longer viewed herself as a lonely traveler. Hers was not a single, isolated voice. There were others in this country who felt as she did. They were working hard to challenge the laws and bring about change. The people whom Sojourner Truth met at the Association would let nothing stand in their way in their quest for freedom.

Sojourner Truth met Olive Gilbert in Northampton, who offered to write her memoirs. He suggested that she dictate her story to him about her early life as a slave in the North. He believed her profound faith in God would be uplifting to many people. In 1850 she and Gilbert published the *Narrative of Sojourner Truth,* which included an introduction by Garrison. None of the bookstores would carry the book, so Sojourner had to support herself by selling copies at abolitionist meetings.

During the next seven years Sojourner became concerned about women's rights. In October 1850, she traveled to Worcester, Massachusetts, to speak at that year's national women's rights convention. In May of 1851 she spoke at a women's rights convention in Akron, Ohio. Afterwards William Lloyd Garrison and his associate Wendell Phillips persuaded Sojourner to speak on behalf of the abolitionist cause and she soon began traveling with other lecturers on tours throughout New England. While traveling on the lecture circuit, she sold many copies of her book, and with proceeds from the sales, she bought a house in Northampton.

In mid-1853, after a successful tour through the Midwest, Sojourner decided to return East and visit members of her family. After enjoying a pleasant stay with her daughters' families, she set out for her house in Northampton. But first she stopped in Andover, Massachusetts, the home of abolitionist writer Harriet Beecher Stowe, who wrote the popular antislavery novel *Uncle Tom's Cabin.* The meeting between Sojourner and Harriet proved to be memorable for both women.

Whenever Sojourner attended an abolitionist or women's rights meeting, she always brought along several copies of her autobiography to sell as well as a new item: postcards that bore her photograph and the legend *I Sell the Shadow to Support the Substance.* She called these cards her *cartes de visite,* which is French for "calling cards." She also brought her "Book of Life," an album in which she collected short notes and autographs from many of the people she met.

In 1857, Sojourner decided to move to Battle Creek, Michigan, a town with strong abolitionist roots. However, she had only a brief time to enjoy the tranquility of her new home. That year, the Supreme Court stunned the North by ruling that Congress did not have the right to pass laws that restricted slavery. It was called the Dred Scott decision. This caused Sojourner to return to the antislavery lecture circuit and tour throughout Indiana, Illinois, and Iowa.

The Civil War broke out on April 12, 1861 when Conferate units attacked the Union troop stationed at Fort Sumter, in Charleston, South Carolina. Sojourner decided to make a tour of the Midwest and seek support for the Union's war effort. Exhausted by the rigors of her tours, she returned home to recuperate. Her daughters and their children had moved to Battle Creek.

Sojourner's strength was momentarily restored after President

Lincoln signed the Emancipation Proclamation, which declared that all slaves in the rebellious Confederate states would be free on January 1, 1863. But Sojourner soon became too ill to work or travel. Before long her family ran into financial difficulties. Word of her dire situation reached the abolitionist newspaper *Anti-Slavery Standard,* and its editor collected donations for her from their readers. This enabled her to buy a small house in Battle Creek.

In the spring of 1864, still just recently recovered from her long illness, Sojourner decided to visit President Abraham Lincoln in Washington, D.C. Accompanied by her grandson, Sam Banks, she boarded a train for the nation's capital, stopping at several towns along the way to give speeches. She reached Washington in September 1864, a little more than a month before Americans were to go to the polls and decide whether Lincoln should be given a second term in office. The president faced strong opposition from the Copperheads, the antiwar faction of the Democratic party, who wanted to sign an immediate peace with the South and leave slavery intact.

On the morning of October 29, 1864, Sojourner joined a group of people waiting in the White House's reception room for their appointment with the president. When she talked to him, Sojourner thanked the president and advised him not to worry about the blustering attacks of his critics. She told him that the people were behind him and would support him in the upcoming election. Lincoln in turn thanked her for the encouragement and then signed her "Book of Life." He wrote, *For Aunty Sojourner Truth, A. Lincoln, Oct. 29, 1864.*

In November, Lincoln was swept back into office by an overwhelming margin, in the wake of several victories by the Union army. By that time, Sojourner had discovered that she greatly enjoyed the busy atmosphere in the capital. Instead of returning to Battle Creek, she decided to remain in Washington and see what she could do to assist the Union's war effort.

Toward the end of 1864, a public welfare organization called the National Freedman's Relief Association asked her to work as a counselor to former slaves who were living in a camp in

Arlington Heights, Virginia. There she educated the freedmen about the need to find work and housing and about other responsibilities that came with their newly won liberty. In 1865, the Freedman's Bureau, a federal relief agency, appointed Sojourner to an administrative position in the Freedman's Hospital in Washington. She did her best to ensure that proper medical care was given to the hospital's African-American patients, who became used to hearing her tell them, "Be Clean. Be Clean." While in Washington, Sojourner also integrated the streetcar system.

Sojourner was still in Washington on the night of April 14, 1865, when Abraham Lincoln was assassinated while watching the performance of a play at Ford's Theater. He was shot by the actor John Wilkes Booth; he died early the next morning. Sojourner was among those who were devastated by his death.

On December 12, 1865, Sojourner and millions of Americans celebrated as Congress ratified the Thirteenth Amendment to the U.S. Constitution. This amendment declared that "neither slavery nor involuntary servitude . . . should exist within the United States or any place subject to their jurisdiction." A little more than two and a half centuries after being established in America, slavery was at last officially abolished.

In 1868, Sojourner began her campaign to persuade Congress to grant land in the West to African-American settlers. Also in 1868, Congress ratified the Fourteenth Amendment of the Constitution, which granted American citizenship to all African-Americans and gave them full civil rights. On March 31, 1870, Sojourner called on the new president of the United States, Ulysses S. Grant, to offer her personal thanks for Congress ratifying the Fifteenth Amendment, giving all Americans, regardless of color, the right to vote. He signed her "Book of Life."

A month later, an historic event took place. On April 26, 1870, Sojourner visited the seventy-three chambers of the capital building to see the senators. Fourteen senators clustered around to sign her book; the others looked on benevolently, talking among themselves. Many regarded Sojourner as a novelty who had survived with dignity all the changes of the past decade. Sen. Charles Summer invited her to his office, where they could speak privately. He advised her to get more signatures on her petition for the Western land grant. In her book he wrote, *Equality of rights is the first of rights. Charles Summer, Senate Chamber, April 26, 1870.*

For long years Sojourner, with her grandson Sammy by her side and her "Book of Life" under her arm, headed north to collect the signatures she needed. Sojourner and Sammy would rise at the crack of dawn to take a carriage to the next meeting place. For hours she gave speeches, answered hecklers, discussed, pleaded, and argued. Never staying long in one place, she relied on friends, acquaintances, and sympathizers to help her on her way. Many times Sojourner thought about her comfortable house and garden in Battle Creek, and about retiring, because she received pay for her work for the Freedman's Bureau and was paying off the small mortgage. But she knew she alone could achieve success in the mission. It was up to Sojourner Truth to win land for her people.

In 1874 Sojourner set out with Sammy for Washington. The pile of petitions was never out of their sight. When they arrived at Senator Summer's office on March 10, they were told that the senator had suffered a heart attack while speaking in Congress and died the same day. Because Sojourner had faced discouragement many times in her life, she knew that, even though she was seventy-seven years old, she would have to fight for the land bill herself in her own way.

Sojourner's last glimmer of hope faded when her grandson Sammy became ill. He survived the trip back to Battle Creek but died in February 1875. Sojourner suffered a minor stroke, leaving her partially paralyzed on one side of her body. She lost much of her hearing. She also developed painful ulcers on her legs that made it difficult and sometimes impossible for her to move.

Sojourner began to recover. Among the first to visit her was Frances Titus, who urged her to update the 1850 edition of the *Narrative*. To the original book, Mrs. Titus wanted to add articles, selections from Sojourner's speeches, and names from the "Book of Life." That spring Sojourner finally agreed to let her update the book. This gave Sojourner another book to sell. When she had no other means of income, book sales helped support her. Seeing her book in print also provided her with a new incentive to travel.

In 1877, according to some accounts, Sojourner's health mysteriously improved. Her hearing returned and her sight sharpened dramatically. Soon after her eightieth birthday, she appeared at a number of meetings supporting women's rights, prison reform, temperance, and the rights of workingmen. In July 1878, at the age of eighty-one, she was one of the three Michigan delegates to the Women's Rights Convention in Rochester.

Late in 1879 Sojourner traveled to Kansas. This was her last, long journey. At the beginning of 1882, she had become gravely ill. The ulcers covering her arms and legs made her too weak to get up from bed. She remained this way for the next year and a half. Sojourner sank into a deep coma and died at 3:00 A.M. on November 26, 1883 in Battle Creek, Michigan.

LIBERTY AND PEACE

This poem was published in Boston in 1784, a few days after Phillis Wheatley's death.

> Lo freedom comes. Th' president muse foretold,
> All eyes th'accomplished prophecy behold:
> Her port described, "She moves divinely fair,
> Olive and laurel bind her golden hair."
> She, the bright progeny of Heaven, descends,
> And every grace her sovereign step attends,
> For now kind Heaven, indulgent to our prayer,
> In smiling peace resolves the din of war.
> Fixed in Columbia her illustrious line,
> And bids in three her future council shine.
> To every realm her portals opened wide,
> Receives from each the full commercial tide.
> Each art and science now with rising charms,
> She welcomes gladly with expanded arms.
> E'en great Britannia sees with dread surprise,
> And from the dazzling splendors turns her eyes.
> Britain, whose navies swept Th' Atlantic o'er,

And thunder sent to every distant shore;
E'en thou, in manners cruel as thou art,
The sword resigned, resume the friendly part.
For Gallia's power espoused Columbia's cause,
And new-born Rome shall give Britannia laws.
Nor unremembered in the grateful stain'
Shall princely Louis' friendly deeds remain;
The generous prince impending vengeance eyes,
Sees the fierce wrong and to the rescue files.
Perish that thirst of boundless power, that drew
On Albions head the curse to tyrants due.
But thou appeased submit to Heaven's decree,
That bids this realm of freedom rival thee.
Now sheathe the sword that bade the brave atone.
With guiltless bold for madness not their own.
Sent from enjoyment of their native shore,
Ill-fated-never to behold her more.
From every kingdom there on Europe's coast
Thronged many troops, their glory, strength, and boast.
With heart-felt pity fair Hibernia saw
Columbia menaced by the Tyrant's law:
On hostile death, all dealt with mutual rage.
The muse's ear hears mother Earth deplore
Her ample surface smoke with kindred gore;
The hostile field destroys the social ties,
And everlasting slumber seals their eyes.
Columbia mourns, the haughty foes deride,
Her treasures plundered and her towns destroyed.
Witness how Charlestown's curling smokes arise,
In sable columns to the clouded skies.
The ample dome, high-wrought with curious toil,
In one sad hour the savage troops despoil.
Descending peace the power of war confounds,
From every tongue celestial peace resounds:
As from the east the mighty king of day,
With rising radiance drives the shades away,
So freedom comes arrayed with charms divine,
And in her train commerce and plenty shine.
Britannia owns her independent reign,
Hibernia, Scotia and the realms of Spain;
And great Germania's ample coast admires
The generous spirit that Columbia fires.
Auspicious Heaven shall fill with favoring gales,
Where e'er Columbia spreads her swelling sails:
To every realm shall peace her charms display,
And heavenly freedom spread her golden ray.

126

Freedom Fighter

Harriet Ross Tubman

HARRIET ROSS TUBMAN
(Born about 1820—Died 1913)

Harriet Tubman was the first African-American woman to be recognized as the "Moses of Her People," and to be recognized as the most daring of freedom fighters. She escaped slavery in 1849, and even though she could not read or write, her efforts helped free over three hundred slaves. She was considered the greatest "conductor" on the Underground Railroad—an organized network of way stations that helped slaves escape from the South to the free states and as far north as Canada.

Harriet Tubman was born Harriet Ross around 1820. She was the sixth of eleven children born to Ben and Harriet Green. As slaves for the Brodas family in Maryland, they all lived in a tiny one-room shack. It had a dirt floor, no windows, and no furniture. There were no beds. The whole family slept on rags and straw spread on the floor. There were no dishes. The slaves' food, which was mostly corn mush, was eaten right from the pot it was cooked in.

When Harriet was still a very small child, she began running errands for Mr. Brodas and his family. She carried messages as far as ten miles away. Soon after she turned five, Harriet was given a new task. Mrs. Brodas put her to work in the mansion, which was called the "big house." Harriet did not know anything about housework, because she had never been inside a real house before—only in the one-room slave shacks—and nobody showed her how to do the things she was supposed to do in the mansion. So Harriet made all kinds of mistakes, and when she made mistakes she was punished.

Harriet's mother begged Mr. Brodas to let her little girl stay home, and he agreed because she was ill. There her mother nursed her back to good health. Harriet's next job, at the age of seven, was looking after Mrs. Brodas's baby. Harriet was so small that she had to sit on the floor and have the baby sit in her lap. The baby was always in her lap except when it was asleep or its mother was feeding it.

Handling such a big responsibility was hard for Harriet. She never had any time to play or be by herself. She was constantly watched by Mr. and Mrs. Brodas. They were very strict with her and the other slaves. They wanted to keep them frightened of them. They did not want the slaves to speak up or fight back or try to escape. But the Brodases could not break the spirit of the slaves. They bravely held religious services, even though that was forbidden. They studied reading and writing in secret. They hid and fed other slaves who were trying to escape to the North.

Harriet heard of many uprisings by the slaves—large and small—taking place in many parts of the South. All of this meant one thing to Harriet, that she was not the only angry slave in America. She knew that someday she would be free and when that day came, she would help bring others to freedom.

Harriet did not hide her feelings. She spoke out fearlessly to other slaves on the plantation, and she refused to smile or make believe she was happy in front of the Brodas family. Mrs. Brodas did not like Harriet's proud, defiant looks so she tried to break the child's spirit. To do so, she hired out nine-year-old Harriet to another family in the country.

These people made her work all day, cleaning house. Then she had to work at night, caring for a baby. For no reason she was punished every day and she was fed only enough food to keep her alive.

After a while, Harriet was little more than skin and bones. She was not able to work anymore. The family in the country thought for sure that Harriet was broken, so they sent her back to the Brodas plantation. Her body was weak and weary, but not her spirit. That was still strong.

Harriet's parents did their best to help her get well. Her

mother nursed her every free moment she had and her father taught her all kinds of amazing and useful things. Even though he had never gone to school, her father was a very wise man. As soon as Harriet was up and about, he took her on Sunday afternoon walks in the woods and along the river.

Part of Harriet's strength came from her brothers and sisters. After a day of working in the fields in the hot sun, they came back to the shack and brought her all the news of the day. They sang songs and told her stories and jokes to make her laugh. They did everything they could to make their little sister happy.

Another part of Harriet's strength came from her faith. Of all the stories in the Bible, the one the slaves liked most was about Moses. He had led the Israelites from slavery. The slaves prayed for a Moses of their own, someone who would lead them to freedom. Harriet believed deeply that the burden on her people would be eased. She believed that they were meant to be free. She believed what she read in the Bible: that all people were equal in the eyes of God.

In the next three years, Harriet grew stronger in body and faith. As soon as she was well Mrs. Brodas hired her out to another master. This one had her do work hard enough for a grown man. She split rails with an axe, hauled wood, and did other heavy jobs. It was difficult but she never gave up, even when it seemed too much to bear.

By the time she was eleven, Harriet was muscular and very strong. She could work as hard and as long as any grown-up. Mr. Brodas saw this and put her to work in the fields. Harriet wore a bandanna—a large handkerchief—on her head. For the rest of her life she would always wear a bandanna. It reminded her of her days as a slave and how far from the fields she had come.

In 1831, new harsher laws were passed. Now, slaves were not allowed to gather in groups. They were not supposed to talk while they worked, and they were never to be on the public roads without a pass from their masters. The rules were made stricter because of an uprising led by a man named Nat Turner.

131

Nat Turner was a slave from Virginia; he was called the Prophet. In the summer of 1831 he led about seventy slaves in a bloody revolt. It took armed troops to stop the revolt and three full months to capture Turner. The slave owners were scared. If a revolt could happen in Virginia, it could happen anywhere. The fear haunted them more and more, and that is why they made stricter laws for the slaves.

But Nat Turner had lit the flame of freedom in many slaves, and Harriet was one of these. One night she told her family that she felt just like Nat Turner did, that it was better to be dead than a slave. Her brother William said he felt that it was better to be alive and free. He told Harriet that he was thinking about taking their freedom for themselves by "riding the Underground Railroad."

People were talking about the "Underground Railroad" that took runaway slaves quickly and safely to the North. It had nothing to do with trains and underground tunnels; it was just a network of good people who risked their lives to help slaves escape. Some of them hid runaways in their cellars, barns, attics, or in secret rooms in their houses. These brave people were called "stationmasters." The hiding places were called "depots" or "stations." Other people took the runaways from one depot to another in a hay wagon, on horseback, or on foot. These people were called "conductors." The runaways themselves were known as "passengers" or "parcel." After William told Harriet about the Underground Railroad, she thought about it all the time. It was this thought that kept Harriet going, that maybe one day she would take a ride to freedom.

When Harriet was fifteen her hope and her life almost ended. One September evening she was sent to the village store. While she was there another slave hurried in, running from his slave master. Harriet and the young boy next to her were told to hold him so the slave master could tie him up. Harriet didn't obey the order and she kept the other boy from doing anything. Suddenly the runaway ran to the door. The slave master leaped to the store counter and, picking up a heavy lead weight, threw it at the runaway. But it missed the

132

man and the heavy piece of metal struck Harriet in the head. She fell to the floor unconscious and for the next couple of months she lay near death.

At first she couldn't eat, and she grew thinner and thinner and slept most of the time. Her wound was healing slowly, but there was a very deep cup in the forehead. It left a scar she would carry for the rest of her life.

Mr. Brodas was sure Harriet was going to die, so he tried to sell her but no one wanted to buy her. Winter came and she was still alive. Her parents were thankful but still worried about her. Harriet could walk, talk, and do light chores around the shack. But sometimes, in the middle of whatever she was doing, she fell asleep. It could happen even while she was saying something. She would simply stop talking, close her eyes, and sleep for a few minutes. Then she would wake up and go on talking as if no time had passed.

The Brodas family was sure that Harriet was half-witted, so they tried much harder to sell her, but she did not want to be sold and sent away from her family. So when the Brodases brought a buyer she would make believe she was having one of her spells, or she would act very stupid. Her family and friends went along with her playacting and nobody was ever interested in buying her.

In time, Harriet's strength returned. She could lift huge, heavy barrels and pull a loaded wagon for miles. She drove the oxen in the fields and plowed from morning to night. It was said that she was stronger than the strongest man in Maryland. It was the strength she would need in the days to come.

Harriet's dream of freedom was still alive, but she had to put it off for a while. In 1844, she married a free African-American man named John Tubman. She hoped that he would help her escape to the North, but the marriage was not happy and they soon parted.

Not long after that, word reached the Brodases' slaves that many of them were going to be sold. Harriet knew the time had come to make the break for freedom. She turned for help to a white woman who lived nearby. This woman had once told

133

her that if she ever needed anything, to come to her. Harriet knew that meant helping her to escape. Without telling anyone she set out for Bucktown, where the white woman lived. The woman gave her a paper with two names on it, and directions to the first house where she would receive aid.

When Harriet reached the first house the woman's husband, who was a farmer, came home in the early evening and in the dark he loaded a wagon. He put Harriet in it, well covered, and drove to the outskirts of another town. Here he told her to get out and directed her to a second station. She was passed along this way, from station to station. She was riding the Underground Railroad, and she didn't stop until she crossed into Pennsylvania.

Now she was free at last. But her heaven wasn't perfect, because she felt like a stranger in a strange land. Her home was down in Maryland with her parents, sisters, and brothers. She decided to make a home in the North and bring them there.

When I found I had crossed that line, I looked at my hands to see if I was the same person. There was such a glory over everything. (Said to her biographer, Sarah H. Bradford, in 1868.)

In the next few years, Harriet made several trips to the South, risking her life to bring others to freedom. She rescued her family, friends, other slaves—more than three hundred men, women, and children. She was loved by the slaves and they called her their "Moses," because she led them through the wilderness and out of bondage.

I started with this idea in my head, "There's two things I've got a right to . . . death or liberty." (Said to her biographer, Sarah H. Bradford, in 1868.)

She was hated by the slave owners, who offered a $40,000 reward for her capture. But Harriet was never caught. She became the most famous conductor on the Underground Railroad. Her favorite saying was "I never ran my train off the track, and I never lost a passenger."

One of her major disappointments was the ultimate failure of John Brown's raid on Harpers Ferry. She had met and aided Brown in recruiting soldiers for this cause. In fact, he called her "General Tubman," and she was always to regard to him, rather than Lincoln, as the emancipator of her people.

In 1860, Harriet began to canvass the nation, appearing at rights. Shortly before the outbreaks of the Civil War, she was forced for a time to leave Canada, but she soon returned to the United States, serving the Union cause openly and actively as nurse, soldier, spy, and scout. She was particularly valuable in this latter capacity, since her work on the "Railroad" had made her thoroughly familiar with much of the terrain.

After the Civil War, she made her home in Auburn, New York. But she never stopped doing good works. In 1869, she married a war veteran. A year earlier, her biography had been written by Sarah Bradford. The proceeds from the sales of the book were given to her to help ease her financial burden.

Despite her many honors and tributes, including a medal from Queen Victoria of England, Harriet spent her last years in poverty. She did not receive a pension until more than thirty years after the close of the Civil War. Awarded twenty dollars a month for the remainder of her life, she used most of this money to help found a place for the aged and needy, later to be called the Harriet Tubman Home.

Harriet died in Auburn in March 1913.

Bank President

Maggie Lena Walker

MAGGIE LENA WALKER
(Born 1867—Died 1934)

Maggie Lena Walker was the first African-American woman bank president. She was the founder and chief executive of the St. Luke Penny Savings Bank in Richmond, Virginia.

Maggie Lena Mitchell was born on July 15, 1867, the daughter of an ex-slave. Her mother, Elizabeth Draper Mitchell, had been freed before the Civil War ended, but chose to remain with her former masters, the Van Lews. In the Van Lews' house, Elizabeth met Eccles Cuthbert, who was a writer and abolitionist. They were attracted to each other and he was the natural father of Maggie Lena. By the time Maggie was born, her mother had married William Mitchell. He was a handsome, mulatto butler, who also worked at the mansion.. When Maggie was small, her stepfather moved his family to a two-story clapboard house. Years later Maggie's parents had a son, whom they named Johnnie.

When Maggie was older, her stepfather was found dead, which caused her mother to work harder than ever to support her two young children. There was never enough money. Maggie's carefree days were over. She had to assume the role of comforter and helpmate to her mother. Although she was only three years older than her brother, she was responsible for caring for him. But Maggie's mother was determined that her daughter would get a good education. She did not want her to be a washwoman like herself.

At age eleven Maggie was baptized by the Reverend Holmes, the pastor of the First African Church. Later Maggie became a Sunday school teacher, because she enjoyed working with little children. On her fourteenth birthday, she joined the Independent Order of St. Luke. At that time, she was one of the youngest members to join. The Order provided for people in need. Maggie volunteered to work there part time. At the same time, she attended the Normal School a few blocks from her home. She studied hard, achieving the highest academic average of the ten students in her class, and received her diploma in 1883.

After her graduation, at age sixteen, Maggie worked part time as an insurance agent for the Women's Union. At the same time, she went to night school to learn bookkeeping. She enjoyed her work in the insurance business, but part-time work was not enough to support her and her family.

Maggie's former high school principal, Ms. Lizzie Knowles, offered her a teaching position at Lancaster School. At that time, it was not uncommon for women to teach without attending college. Maggie enthusiastically accepted the offer and began teaching the fall of 1883. She taught school for three years, but teaching was not all she did. She continued to work part time for the Women's Union, to take courses in accounting, and to volunteer at St. Luke. She enjoyed all these activities.

After teaching a while, Maggie married Armstead Walker on September 14, 1886. Armstead worked with his father, who was a prominent builder of some of the finest homes in Richmond. Marriage signaled the end of Maggie's teaching career, but it did not keep the energetic lady from working at St. Luke. At a time when women were expected to stay home, Mrs. Walker was working full time. Her work became a labor of love.

Mrs. Walker was eager to have a baby. Her firstborn came into life with a wretched struggle. She thought that he would surely die. She, too, was close to death, but careful nursing brought them both back. For five months she was confined to bed, gradually regaining her strength. The baby, Russell Eccles Thomas, also grew in health and strength. Mrs. Walker was happy. Her second son, Armstead Mitchell Walker, was born in 1893 and died during infancy. It was a terrible blow for Maggie and her husband. Nonetheless, they were grateful that Russell had survived. Then in August 1894, their last child, Melvin Dewitt Walker, was born. The Walker boys had a good life. Armstead was a successful contractor and Maggie was a successful businesswoman.

In 1899, the Independent Order of St. Luke held its thirty-second annual convention in Hinton, West Virginia. At this convention Mrs. Walker was elected grand secretary. This meant she would run the business, which was losing money and members. She surprised the members by agreeing to serve at one-third salary. She couldn't let the Order die because people needed the kind of help the Order provided—for example, insurance to help pay for funeral services and burials.

She started traveling a lot to organize councils, which were like little clubs, encouraging new members to join. When Mrs. Walker talked everyone listened. She was a tall, heavy, buxom woman, with a deep, mellow voice. Her ability to speak with confidence, knowledge, and charm became her trademark.

Due to her brilliant business ability and her magnetic personality the Order became successful. The members were from all walks of life, from maids to doctors, and the business included insurance, a printing press, and a small newspaper. She later saw the need for an Educational Loan Fund that would aid students who wanted to go to college. Members could borrow money from the Fund to pay for their children's education. She also reorganized the Juvenile Branch that had been organized by her in 1895.

The *St. Luke Herald* was the newsletter published by St. Luke to keep members aware of what the Order was doing, as well as to speak out against unfairness to African-Americans. One section of the newsletter was devoted to children's work. They wrote stories, poems, and articles for the newspaper.

It was felt that one of Mrs. Walker's best ideas was the St. Luke Penny Savings Bank. She believed that people could turn "nickels into dollars" by pooling their money and lending it out. Her dream of a bank, owned and operated by African-Americans, became a reality on November 2, 1903. Mrs.

141

Walker became president and founder of the first African-American bank. People came from as far away as New York to make deposits in the new bank. Total receipts for the opening day were $9,430.44. People opened Christmas savings accounts for a penny or a nickel a week.

Mrs. Walker would attend Juvenile Society meetings and encourage the young people to work hard, keep themselves clean, go to church regularly, and save money. Each child was given a bank in which to put his/her pennies. The youth had a special day called Sunshine Day where they send out a ray of sunshine by visiting the sick, running an errand, or taking food to a needy family. Mrs. Walker set high standards for adults as well as children.

Mrs. Walker nearly always caused a great sensation as she rode through town in her chauffeur-driven limousine. It was a most uncommon sight to see an African-American chauffeur driving another African-American. Seeing the twosome really inspired the young people.

In 1911 Virginia passed a law that required all banks to separate from fraternal organizations. So St. Luke Penny Savings Bank had to cut its ties with St. Luke Order.

In 1915 a tragedy hit the family. Mrs. Walker's son Russell accidently shot his father, because he thought that he was a prowler. He was arrested for his father's murder. Five months later, in June, the jurors returned a verdict of "not guilty." But members of St. Luke felt that Russell's trial and the publicity was a disgrace to the organization's good name, so they demanded Mrs. Walker's resignation.

Still weakened and saddened by the tragedy, Mrs. Walker somehow gained the strength to fight back. She reminded the members of her dedication, her hard work, and the progress that had been made under her leadership. After her speech the quiet and suspense were broken by cheers and applause. She received a standing ovation and remained grand secretary for many more years. She had overcome another obstacle.

At one time four generations of the Walker family lived together under one roof. The two-story house was deeper than it was wide. It grew until there were fourteen rooms. Mrs. Walker's mother, Elizabeth Mitchell, also lived in the house— she who had been a slave, a servant and washwoman; the woman who had lived and toiled for her two children, Maggie and Johnnie. Those early years had been such a struggle compared to the comfortable life she now had in her daughter's home. Elizabeth Mitchell died on February 12, 1922, leaving cherished memories for the whole family. Russell died almost two years later, on November 23, 1923. He had never fully recovered from his father's death. Despite the loving efforts of his mother, wife, and daughter, he became very depressed and drank too much.

Mrs. Walker had injured her kneecap in 1908 and she was finding it increasingly difficult to bear the pain in her leg. She was later confined to a wheelchair. An elevator was installed in the rear of the house and the car was adjusted so that the wheelchair could fit into it. Mrs. Walker overcame poverty and paralysis. She was totally devoted to uplifting people. She encouraged racial pride, thrift, and self-help through her work with the Independent Order of St. Luke and the St. Luke Penny Savings Bank. The bank still exists as the Consolidated Bank and Trust Company. It is the oldest continuously operating minority-owned bank in America.

Maggie Lena Walker died in 1934.

Journalist

Ida B. Wells-Barnett

IDA B. WELLS-BARNETT
(Date of birth unknown—Died 1931)

Ida Wells-Barnett was the first African-American woman to crusade against lynching of African-Americans. She was born in Holly Springs, Mississippi and she struggled to gain an education. When she was a teenager, both of her parents died within twenty-four hours of each other, leaving her with several younger brothers and sisters to care for. Lying about her age, Ms. Wells became a teacher and sole supporter of her brothers and sisters. She lost her teaching job after she criticized the inadequate schools for African-Americans in Memphis. Later she became a full-time journalist and co-owner of *Freespeech*, a Memphis weekly, and the *Head Light*.

Ms. Wells was educated at Rusk University and was one of the few women in the South who engaged in a vigorous campaign against the lynching practices common at that time. She was affiliated with several newspapers, most prominently as the editor of *Freespeech*.

One cold night in March 1892, a mob of cursing, shouting white men broke into the jail at Memphis, hustled three African-American prisoners out into an open field, and riddled them with bullets. The African-Americans, friends of Ms. Wells, were lynched, not for rape of a white woman, but for the crimes of being "uppity" and "too successful" in the small grocery business. Ms. Wells, writing under the pen name "Iola," published a detailed exposé on the mob and its dirty work in *Freespeech*. Her investigative report also proved that most "rapes" that led to lynching were affairs between consenting adults. The very night that the exposé appeared, a mob invaded her office and destroyed the printing equipment and all the copies of the newspaper that it could find. A determined search for Ms. Wells was made, but her friends had hidden her away from danger.

After her press was destroyed, Ms. Wells went to New York and joined the staff of the *New York Age,* edited by T. Thomas Fortune. With the encouragement of such men as Frederick Douglass and William Monroe Trotter, Ms. Wells publicized the facts of lynching.

After lecturing in the United States and England, Ms. Wells married Ferdinand Lee Barnett, a lawyer, editor, the publisher of the first black newspaper in Chicago (the *Chicago Conservator*), and an opponent of Booker T. Washington's conciliatory policies. She and her husband fought untiringly for equal rights in America. As chairman of the Anti-Lynching Bureau of the Afro-American Council, she related statistics that proved Frederick Douglass's contention that protecting the virtue of white Southern women was not the motivation for lynching.

In 1895 she published "The Red Record: Tabulated Statistics and Alleged Causes of Lynchings in the United States, 1892-1893-1894." The pamphlet was "Respectfully submitted to 19th Century Civilization in the Land of the Free and the Home of the Brave." It included details of lynchings and other information that underscored the irony of the phrase. This pioneering effort in the field of statistics on lynchings was a forerunner of similar work done at the Tuskegee Institute and by the NAACP. Mrs. Wells-Barnett also wrote several other pamphlets and articles as she continued to speak across the United States and in Europe.

In 1898, Mrs. Wells-Barnett headed a group that protested to President William McKinley about lynchings. She said that "nowhere in the civilized world, except in the United States, do men go out in bands of fifty to five thousand to hunt down, shoot, hang, or burn to death a single individual, unarmed and absolutely powerless." The group declared that if the United States could protect Americans in foreign countries, it could defend citizens at home. This plea for justice proved as futile as had Douglass's earlier demands to Presidents Johnson and Harrison.

Mrs. Wells-Barnett worked with W. E. B. Du Bois against Booker T. Washington's policy of accommodation. Citing mob violence against African-American people, she declared that Washington was wrong in saying that the African-American could achieve his rights through economic power. She worked again with Du Bois in founding the National Association for the Advancement of Colored People. After the Springfield, Illinois, riot of 1908, Oswald Garrison Villard (William Lloyd Garrison's grandson) asked concerned African-Americans and whites to meet to discuss the racial crisis. Booker T. Washington refused to attend, but at a second conference, despite his opposition, the NAACP organization took form.

After having become chairman of the Anti-Lynching Bureau, Mrs. Wells-Barnett organized and became the first president of the African-American Fellowship League in 1908. Five years later, her social work began to center around Chicago, where she was appointed probation officer. She left this post in 1915, having been elected vice-president of the Chicago Equal Rights League.

Ida B. Wells-Barnett in her time was perhaps the most famous African-American female journalist in the country. She was a correspondent for the *Detroit Plain Dealer*, the *Christian Index*, and the *People's Choice*, and had written for the *New York Age*, the *Indianapolis World*, *The Gate City Press* (Mo.), *The Little Rock Sun*, *The Memphis Watchman*, *The Chattanooga Justice*, and *The Fisk Herald*. She was a columnist for *Our Women and Children*, edited by the author of *Men of Mark*, William J. Simmons. Twice Mrs. Wells-Barnett had been secretary of the Afro-American Press Association.

Mrs. Wells-Barnett continued her crusading activities until her death in 1931. Her forty-year fight for fair treatment for African-Americans earned her a prominent place in the ranks of American leaders.

149

Poet

Phillis Wheatley

PHILLIS WHEATLEY
(Born 1753—Died 1784)

Phillis Wheatley was the first African-American woman to attain literary distinction. In 1761, at the heart of the New England trade in rum, tobacco, sugar, and slaves, was the Port of Boston. Here a small, fragile, and very dark-complexioned child was placed on the slave block. Sheltered from the New England weather by only a few rags on her naked body, this little girl of seven or eight was still without her permanent front teeth when she was put up for sale to the highest bidder. She was sold like a bundle of hay or a cord of wood to John Wheatley, merchant and tailor.

The merchant gave the child to his wife, Susannah, whose motherly instincts overcame her natural reticence. The frail girl was pampered and petted back into a semblance of health, by the woman who came as close to being a mother to the kidnapped African-American girl as the circumstances would permit.

Phillis was born in Senegal in 1753. She was brought to the United States as a slave from Africa. She was given her name from Mrs. Wheatley. Phillis received her early education in the household of her master. Her interest in writing stemmed from her reading of the Bible and the classics under the guidance of the Wheatleys' daughter, Mary. The Wheatleys also had a son, Nathaniel.

Mary asked her mother to give Phillis to her for her very own, so she and her brother could continue to teach her. They made up a little bed in one corner of Mary's room for Phillis. Mary became devoted to Phillis. During this time in Boston it was uncommon for a girl to be able to write, but Mary had more education than most fifteen-year-old girls. Girls who did not have to work stayed at home and learned cooking, housekeeping, and needlework from their mothers. The more fortunate were given a year or two of "finishing" in the Young Ladies' Seminary.

Phillis proved to the Wheatleys that she could grasp things very quickly. Nathaniel decided to teach her Latin. Within a matter of months, Phillis was translating Homer's poetry from Latin into English. She continued to grow and learn. Each day it became more apparent that she was no ordinary child. Phillis, too, began to realize that she was different from other slaves.

Mr. Wheatley reprimanded Phillis for wasting time writing poetry, but she felt he would not object when she was in her own room at night. Even though things were happening around her, they were of no concern to Phillis, because she continued to stretch her mind in new studies. She wrote poetry in the privacy of her room and spent pleasant hours reading to Mrs. Wheatley.

At age thirteen, Phillis was rapidly leaving childhood behind. She was growing tall and slender with an aristocratic look about her.

From the beginning Phillis received recognition for her poetry. She wrote a poem for the king of England the night Boston celebrated the repeal of the Stamp Act. The king received the poem and instructed Lord Dartmouth of the Royal Court to send a copy to the governor so he could make sure the poem was written by Phillis Wheatley. After extensive questioning it was agreed by Thomas Hutchinson, royal governor of the Massachusetts Colony, and the seventeen judges in attendance that she wrote the poem. Phillis was elevated to the status of a minor celebrity.

In late October 1770 a broadside of Phillis's poetry was published. It was the first time an African-American woman had been published. In fact, she was only the second woman ever to be published in America. In the next four months, it was reprinted once in Newport, four more times in Boston, once in New York, and once in Philadelphia. It was received with overwhelming enthusiasm. Phillis's first book of poetry was published in 1773, while she was in London. It was entitled *Poems on Various Subjects, Religious and Moral.* In London she was the guest of the countess of Huntington.

Shortly after Phillis was freed by Rev. John Lathrop in 1778, she married John Peters, an intelligent but irresponsible free African-American man. Their first child was a girl whom they named Mary, and their second child was a boy whom they named George Washington Peters. Their third child was born nearly five weeks early and was very sickly. They named her Eliza.

In 1783 a dysentery epidemic struck and Phillis's son and her oldest daughter died. Phillis survived her own serious illness, but was drained of the joy of living. She no longer thrilled to the sound of birds singing. She ate without tasting anything. Eliza became the focus of Phillis's existence, her only reason for living.

Later Phillis's husband was sentenced to an indeterminate time in debtors' prison. Phillis tried unsuccessfully to get a job as a governess or tutor. At last she resorted to looking for cleaning work, but few people could afford to hire anyone. She had not heard from her husband for more than a year, since he had been transferred to the prison on Castle Island for his participation in an escape plan discovered by one of the guards.

Finally, Phillis was able to find a job as a housekeeper. Her hours were from seven in the morning until seven at night, but it was often nine or later before she and Eliza started home. Phillis was often very fatigued by the time they walked the long distance home. She hoped this winter would not be as bad as last year.

By early November 1784, Phillis found herself so weary that just taking another step or lifting a broom became a formidable task. She tried to save her precious energy for her job. Eliza waited on her hand and foot when they were home. Despair flooded Phillis. Just taking care of Eliza was more than she could manage these days. But even though she was sick, she continued to work.

One day she was fired from her job when she broke a vase. Her employer, Mrs. McGuire, felt she was in no condition to work. Phillis made it home, but she did not know how long she lay in bed. Her days had become an endless succession of pain and futility. She was conscious only that Eliza's emaciated body, aflame with fever, lay huddled next to her, and an occasional whimper was the only sound she heard from her for hours at a time. Finally opening her eyes, she realized the fireplace was dark and she had burned the last of the wood yesterday, or was it the day before?

It was dark when Phillis awakened again. The cold was so intense she could see white rings when she breathed. She reached for Eliza, but her daughter lay peacefully still. She searched frantically for a pulse but there was none. She reflected on her thirty-one years of life. She touched her daughter and grasped the stiffening fingers. Eliza was where she would never be cold or hungry again. On December 5, 1784 Phillis closed her eyes finally as a beautiful sensation of peace and warmth crept over her.

It was felt that Phillis wrote her own best epitaph:

> But when these shades of time are chased away,
> And darkness ends in everlasting day,
> On what seraphic pinions shall we move,
> And view the landscapes in the realms above?
> There shall my tongue in heav'nly transport glow;
> No more to tell of Damon's tender sighs,
> Or rising radiance of Aurora's eyes,
> For nobler themes demand a nobler strain,
> And purer language on th'ethereal plane.
> Cease, gentle music! the solemn gloom of night
> Now seals the fair creation from my sight.

A few days after Phillis's death, one of her finest poems was published. "Liberty and Peace," inspired by the end of the

Revolutionary War, was a fitting conclusion to the rich and creative life she had led. She came from an unknown village in West Africa and her burial place in Boston, with an unmarked grave, remains unknown. On February 1, 1985, Governor Michael Dukakis proclaimed it Phillis Wheatley Day, for the woman who is recognized as the mother of black literature in this country.

Television Host

Oprah Winfrey

OPRAH GAIL WINFREY
(Born 1954—   )

Oprah Winfrey was the first African American woman to host a nationally syndicated talk show. She was also the first African American woman to produce her own talk show and to own a production company.

Oprah was born on January 29, 1954, in Kosciusko, Mississippi, to Vernita Lee and Vernon Winfrey. Her name was supposed to have been *Orpah,* a biblical figure in the Book of Ruth, but the letters were reversed and her name was recorded as Oprah Gail Winfrey. Her parents, who were not married, separated when she was very young and Oprah lived with her grandmother, Hattie Mae, on the farm she owned in Mississippi. Hattie Mae raised chickens and pigs, and sold produce to earn money to buy necessities. She also made all of her clothes by hand. Since there were no other children within walking distance of their farm, Oprah experienced feelings of isolation and loneliness, but she always knew she was loved.

Oprah loved to talk and play-act. She used the animals on the farm and grownups that visited her grandmother as her audience. At Faith United Methodist Church, Oprah often amazed the congregation with her performances, reciting speeches during Christmas and Easter programs.

Oprah's grandmother's stern and strict discipline gave her stable roots, taught her how to reason, and made her a strong person. Oprah was a very smart child; her grandmother taught her to read by the age of three. When she started kindergarten she was skipped to the first grade, then later, to the second grade. By the age of six, Oprah was in the third grade.

Vernita, Oprah's mother, was only an eighteen year-old farm girl when Oprah was born, and her father was a twenty-two year-old serviceman, stationed in Alabama. Her mother left Alabama and went to Milwaukee, Wisconsin, to find a job and her father stayed in the army. Oprah's mother visited her periodically on the farm when she could afford the trip.

When Oprah was six, her mother moved her to Milwaukee to live with her. Vernita worked hard to maintain a home for Oprah and herself with income from welfare and domestic work. During different periods, Oprah was shifted back and forth between her parents. At the age of eight, Vernita sent Oprah to live with her father and his wife, Zelma, in Nashville, Tennessee. While in Nashville, Oprah performed at her father's church, Faith United. When Oprah was nine, her mother decided that Oprah should live with her again, this time with her stepsister and brother, so she moved Oprah back to Milwaukee.

Many times when Oprah's mother had to be away from home, she left Oprah in the care of male babysitters. It was during these times that Oprah was sexually abused. Oprah was afraid to tell her mother about what was happening to her because she thought she would be blamed and/or punished. These experiences later inspired Oprah to give time and money to help youngsters who are confused and misdirected. The death of a four year-old girl in Chicago who had been molested, strangled, and then discarded in Lake Michigan, prompted Oprah to stand up for the children of this country. She donated money to child advocacy groups and used her talk show as a forum for discussion of child abuse.

By the time Oprah entered Lincoln High School, some of her teachers recognized that she was not being challenged intellectually. One of these teachers, Gene Abrams, helped her to get a full scholarship to Nicolet High School, which was an exclusive private school located in one of Milwaukee's wealthy suburban areas. The school was about twenty-five miles from her home. Oprah continued to excel in her schoolwork and made many friends, but she felt frustrated by the barriers that poverty seemed to place in her path. This along with other things happening to her at school caused her to have very serious behavioral problems and her grades suffered. She started stealing money from her mother's purse, staying out past her curfew, and dating many boys. During these difficult times, at the age of fourteen, Oprah became pregnant and gave birth to a premature baby that died soon afterward. Her mother gave up and sent Oprah to live with her father in Nashville.

Oprah's father was a respected member of his community. He owned his own barbershop, which he later expanded to house a small grocery store. He also served as deacon at his church. From the beginning of Oprah's return to her father, he put her under the strictest guidance. This was a different situation from the one she had experienced with her mother, who expected her to do what she said, not what she did. From this time forth, Oprah's life changed dramatically because her father provided structure for her life, and he stressed hard work and discipline as a means of self-improvement. Her father believed that a good education was the key to Oprah's successful future.

After a shaky beginning, Oprah began to display the same precocious characteristics she had exhibited as a child. Once again she started to excel in school. She became involved in extracurricular activities, such as speech and drama, and was a member of the student council. She became president of the student council, and was invited by President Richard Nixon to attend the White House Conference on Youth. Oprah excelled behind the podium and on the stage; she loved the limelight. At age sixteen, she was voted the most popular girl in her class.

Later, she won an oratorical contest sponsored by the Elks Club and received a scholarship that she used to attend Tennessee State University. Oprah also won the Miss Fire Prevention Contest and on her way to pick up prizes she ran into John Heidelberg, a local disc jockey. From this meeting, while still in high school, Oprah was offered a part-time job as a reporter on WVOL, a local radio station in Nashville.

Oprah was crowned Miss Black Nashville and Miss Black

Tennessee, and was a contestant in the Miss Black America pageant. As a result of winning these titles Oprah was offered a job as a reporter at the local CBS television station, an affiliate of WTVF-TV, where she co-anchored the evening news. In 1971, Oprah became Nashville's first African American female co-anchor. She worked in this position until she left college. Shortly thereafter, in 1976, she was offered a job at WJZ-TV, the ABC affiliate in Baltimore, Maryland. From 1976 to 1983 she lived in Baltimore, progressing from news anchor to co-host of the show, "People Are Talking" with Richard Sher. With Oprah as co-host the program's popularity grew. It was in Baltimore at WJZ that Oprah met Gayle King Bumpus, a fellow employee who later became her best friend.

In 1984 Oprah moved to Chicago to host *A.M. Chicago*. During this time, the program expanded in length from thirty minutes to one hour. The following year, the show was renamed "The Oprah Winfrey Show." On September 8, 1986, the show was syndicated nationally and Oprah founded Harpo, Inc., her own production company ("Harpo" is Oprah spelled backwards). She purchased a block-long building in downtown Chicago that included a production studio containing three sound stages and offices. That same year she was voted by *Ebony* magazine's annual readers' poll as the most admired black woman. In 1989, *Ms.* magazine chose Oprah as Woman of the Year. Oprah later expanded her production company and purchased the screen rights to several best-selling books, many by African American authors.

Oprah's father constantly reminded her that without a college diploma, her success was incomplete. In 1986 Oprah returned to Tennessee State University to complete the requirements for her degree. She received her diploma during the 1987 commencement exercise where she was the speaker. She announced at the graduation that she was going to endow ten annual scholarships in her father's name to help educate students at Tennessee State University.

In 1985 Oprah played the part of Sofia in *The Color Purple*, a

164

movie based on the novel by Alice Walker and directed by Steven Spielberg. Oprah was nominated for an Academy Award for her supporting role in the movie. She also played a leading role in the film version of Richard Wright's novel, *Native Son*, playing the part of Bigger Thomas' mother. In 1989 she served as co-executive producer for and starred as Mattie Michael in the made-for-television movie, *The Women of Brewster Place*, based on the Gloria Naylor novel. She appeared with her best friend, Gayle, in a syndicated prime-time special, *Just Between Friends*. In 1991 Oprah testified before the Senate Judiciary Committee to propose a bill providing for a national screening device for employees convicted of sexual abuse against children. Just two years later, she starred in the made-for-television move, *There Are No Children Here*. Because of this production, President Clinton signed the Oprah Bill, a law designed to protect children from abuse. Essentially, the bill provided for the development of a database containing information on convicted child abusers.

Oprah has won many awards for her work in television and film, including the Horatio Alger Award and The Peabody Award. In 1994 she was inducted into the TV Hall of Fame. At the 1995 Daytime Emmy Awards, *The Oprah Winfrey Show* won its seventh Emmy for Best Talk Show, and Oprah won the Emmy for Best Daytime Television Host.

Oprah has received many other awards for her humanitarian efforts. In 1986, Baltimore honored Oprah with the city's first Celebrity Award. That same year, she formed her own production company, HARPO Productions, Inc., because of her love for acting and her desire to provide quality entertainment.

In 1988, the road that runs in front of her childhood home was renamed Oprah Winfrey Road. In 1996, she established her book club with the intent to rejuvenate the public's interest in literature. Not surprisingly, nearly all of her book club selections have become instant bestsellers. As a result, the American Library Association even selected her as a "celebrity reader" to help promote reading.

Among her other accomplishments, Oprah created the

Vernon Winfrey Scholarships to help educate students at Tennessee University. She also established a one million-dollar scholarship fund at Morehouse College. In addition, she received four Image Awards from the National Association for the Advancement of Colored People (NAACP).

Most recently, Oprah starred as Sethe in HARPO's production of *Beloved,* adapted from Toni Morrison's Pulitzer Prize-winning novel. She has also developed her own website, *Oprah.com,* which contains chat and message boards, biographical information on Oprah herself, and details on past and future show topics. Her latest endeavor is *O Magazine,* designed to be a women's personal growth guide. *O Magazine* shows women how to become more confident, and gives them the tools they need to reach and explore their dreams. Overall, the magazine serves as a catalyst in transforming women's lives.

In 2000, Oprah was a recipient at the Salute to Greatness Award ceremony held in honor of Dr. Martin Luther King, Jr., during his birthday celebration in Atlanta, Georgia. Oprah also established a Little Sisters program in Chicago's Cabrini Green housing projects, and devoted two afternoons each month counseling young women on not getting pregnant and staying in school.

The Oprah Show is currently in syndication all over the country. Oprah continues to provide hope, inspiration, and motivation for all people—young and old, black and white, rich and poor—through her multiple media outlets and charitable organizations.

FURTHER SUGGESTED READING

Allen, William G. *Wheatley, Banneker, and Horton: With Selections from the Poetical Works of Wheatley and Horton.* Ayer Co. Publishers, 1970.

Anderson, LaVere. *Mary McLeod Bethune: A Teacher with a Dream.* Garrard Publishing Co., 1976.

Aylesa. *American Women Who Scored Firsts.* Watts, 1958.

Bains, Rae. *Harriet Tubman: The Road to Freedom.* Troll Associated, 1982.

Bentley, Judith. *Harriet Tubman.* Watts, 1990.

Bernard, Jacqueline. *Journey Toward Freedom: The Story of Sojourner Truth.* Norton, 1967.

Biracree, Tom. *Althea Gibson.* Chelsea House, 1989.

Bowie, Walter Russell. *Women of Light.* Harper, 1963.

Bradford, Sarah H. *Harriet Tubman: The Moses of Her People.* Peter Smith, 1981.

Branch, Muriel. *Miss Maggie: A Biography of Maggie Lena Walker.* Marlborough House Publishing Co., 1984.

Brooks, Gwendolyn. *Report from Part One: An Autobiography.* Broadside Press, 1972.

Brown, Patricia L. and Francis Ward. *To Gwen with Love: A Tribute to Gwendolyn Brooks.* Johnson Chi, 1971.

Brownmiller, Susan. *Shirley Chisholm: A Biography.* Doubleday, 1970.

Burt, Olive Wooley. *Black Women of Valor.* J. Messner, 1974.

Carroll, Diahann and Ross Firestone. *Diahann!* Little, Brown, 1986.

Carruth, Ella Kaiser. *She Wanted to Read: The Story of Mary McLeod Bethune.* Abingdon Press, 1966.

Celsi, Teresa Noel. *Rosa Parks and the Montgomery Bus Boycott.* Millbrook Press, 1991.

Chisholm, Shirley. *The Good Fight.* Harper and Row, 1973.

Conrad, Earl. *Harriet Tubman.* Associated Publishers, 1943.

Dabney, Wendell Phillips. *Maggie L. Walker and the I. O. of Saint Luke: The Woman and Her Work.* The Dabney Publishing Co., 1972.

Duffy, Susan. *Shirley Chisholm: A Bibliography of Writings by and about Her.* Scarecrow Press, 1988.

Fauset, Arthur Huff. *Sojourner Truth: God's Faithful Pilgrim.* Russell and Russell, 1971.

Friese, Kal. *Rosa Parks: The Movement Organizes.* Silver Burdett Press, 1990.

Gibson, Althea. *I Always Wanted to Be Somebody.* W. H. Allen, 1958.

Gilbert, Olive. *Narrative of Sojourner Truth.* Ayer Co. Publishers, 1968.

———. *Narrative of Sojourner Truth: A Bondswoman of Olden Time.* Johnson Publishing Co., 1970.

Grant, Matthew G. *Harriet Tubman.* Children's Press, 1974.

Greenfield, Eloise. *Mary McLeod Bethune.* HarperCollins Children's Books, 1977.

———. *Rosa Parks.* HarperCollins Children's Books, 1973.

Halasa, Malu. *Mary McLeod Bethune*. Chelsea House, 1989.

Haskins, James. *Barbara Jordan*. Dial Press, 1977.

———. *Fighting Shirley Chisholm*. Dial Press, 1975.

Hicks, Nancy. *The Honorable Shirley Chisholm: Congresswoman from Brooklyn*. Lion Books, 1977.

Holt, Rackham. *Mary McLeod Bethune: A Biography*. Doubleday, 1964.

Jackson, Carlton. *Hattie: The Life of Hattie McDaniel*. Madison Books, 1990.

Jacobs, Linda. *Wilma Rudolph: Run for Glory*. EMC Corp., 1975.

Jordan, Barbara. *Barbara Jordan: A Self-Portrait*. Doubleday, 1979.

Kent, George E. *A Life of Gwendolyn Brooks*. University Press of Kentucky, 1990.

Krass, Peter. *Sojourner Truth*. Chelsea House, 1988.

Lindstrom, Aletha Jane. *Sojourner Truth: Slave, Abolitionist, Fighter for Women's Rights*. J. Messner, 1980.

Macdonald, Fiona. *A Chance to Learn*. Watts, 1990.

———. *Working for Equality*. Watts, 1989.

McKissack, Patricia C. *Mary McLeod Bethune: A Great American Educator*. Children's Press, 1985.

Melham, D. H. *Gwendolyn Brooks: Poetry and the Heroic Voice*. University Press of Kentucky, 1987.

Meltzer, Milton. *Mary McLeod Bethune: Voice of Black Hope*. Viking Children's Books, 1987.

Meriwether, Louise. *Don't Ride the Bus on Monday: The Rosa Parks Story*. Prentice Hall, 1973.

Meyer, Linda D. *Harriet Tubman: They Called Me Moses*. Parenting Press, Inc., 1988.

Miller, R. Baxter. *Langston Hughes and Gwendolyn Brooks: A Reference Guide.* G. K. Hall, 1978.

Mootry, Maria K. *A Life Distilled: Gwendolyn Brooks, Her Poetry and Fiction.* University of Illinois Press, 1987.

Newman, Shirlee Petkin. *Marian Anderson: Lady from Philadelphia.* Westminster Press, 1965.

Ortiz, Victoria. *Sojourner Truth: A Self-Made Woman.* Lippincott, 1974.

Parks, Rosa. *Rosa Parks: My Story.* Dial Books, 1992.

Pauli, Hertha. *Her Name Was Sojourner Truth.* Appleton, 1962.

Peare, Catherine Owens. *Mary McLeod Bethune.* Vanguard, 1951.

Peterson, Helen Stone. *Sojourner Truth: Fearless Crusader.* Barrard Publishing Co., 1972.

Petry, Ann Lane. *Harriet Tubman: Conductor on the Underground Railroad.* HarperCollins Children's Books, 1955.

Radford, Ruby Lorraine. *Mary McLeod Bethune.* Rosier, 1973.

Richmond, M. A. *Bid the Vassal Soar: Interpretive Essays on the Life and Poetry of Phillis Wheatley and Joe Moses Horton.* Howard University Press, 1974.

Roberts, Naurice. *Barbara Jordan: The Great Lady from Texas.* Children's Press, 1984.

Robinson, William Henry. *Phillis Wheatley and Her Writings.* Garland, 1984.

———. *Phillis Wheatley in the Black American Beginnings.* Broadside Press, 1975.

Rudolph, Wilma. *Wilma: The Story of Wilma Rudolph.* New American Library, 1977.

Scheader, Catherine. *Shirley Chisholm: Teacher and Congresswoman.* Enslow Publishers, 1990.

Shaw, Harry B. *Gwendolyn Brooks*. Twayne Publishers, 1980.

Sims, Janet L. *Marian Anderson: An Annotated Bibliography and Discography*. Greenwood Press, 1981.

Sterling, Dorothy. *Black Foremothers: Three Lives*. Feminist Press, 1988.

Stern, Emma Gelders. *Mary McLeod Bethune*. Knopf, 1957.

Swift, Hildegarde Hoyt. *Railroad to Freedom*. Harcourt Brace, 1932.

Taylor, M. W. *Harriet Tubman*. Chelsea House, 1991.

Tedards, Anne. *Marian Anderson*. Chelsea House, 1988.

Tobias, Tobi. *Marian Anderson*. HarperCollins Children's Books, 1972.

Vehanen, Kosti. *Marian Anderson, a Portrait*. Greenwood Press, 1970.

Wells, Ida B. *Crusade for Justice: The Autobiography of Ida B. Wells*. University of Chicago Press, 1970.

Wheatley, Phillis. *The Collected Works of Phillis Wheatley*. Oxford University Press, 1988.

————. *Life and Works of Phillis Wheatley*. Ayer Co. Publishers, 1969.

Williams, Sylvia. *Leontyne Price: Opera Superstar*. Children's Press, 1984.

Wilson, Beth P. *Giants for Justice: Bethune, Randolph, and King*. Harcourt Brace Jovanovich, 1978.

Printed in the United States
1737